Piaget's Conception of Evolution

Piaget's Conception of Evolution

Beyond Darwin and Lamarck

JOHN G. MESSERLY

Foreword by
Richard J. Blackwell

ROWMAN & LITTLEFIELD PUBLISHERS, INC.
Lanham • Boulder • New York • London

ROWMAN & LITTLEFIELD PUBLISHERS, INC.

Published in the United States of America
by Rowman & Littlefield Publishers, Inc.
4720 Boston Way, Lanham, Maryland 20706

3 Henrietta Street
London WC2E 8LU, England

British Cataloging in Publication Information Available

Library of Congress Cataloging-in-Publication Data

Messerly, John G. (John Gerard), 1955–
Piaget's conception of evolution : beyond Darwin and Lamarck /
John G. Messerly.
p.   cm.
Includes bibliographical references and index.
1. Piaget, Jean, 1896—Views on evolution. 2. Evolution.
I. Title.
BF109.P5M47   1996   155.4'13'092—dc20   96–13049   CIP

ISBN 0–8476–8242–0 (cloth : alk. paper)
ISBN 0–8476–8243–9 (pbk. : alk. paper)

Printed in the United States of America

♾™ The paper used in this publication meets the minimum requirements of
American National Standard for Information Sciences—Permanence of
Paper for Printed Library Materials, ANSI Z39.48–1984.

To Richard J. Blackwell
an exemplar of moral and intellectual virtue

Bringuier: I wonder if what you attack in philosophy isn't what is called metaphysics?

Piaget: Yes, of course . . .

Bringuier: But isn't metaphysics, like the religious turn of mind or mysticism, a sign of one's longing for unity? That's what I meant about philosophy. One can't turn up one's nose at it too quickly, because the need exists. [Humans have] a need for unity.

Piaget: But, to me, the search for unity is much more substantial than the affirmation of unity; the need and the search, and the idea that one is working at it . . .

Conversations with Bringuier

Contents

    Biology and Knowledge   84
    Behavior: The Motor of Evolution   93

5   Psychogenesis and the History of Science: 105
    Piaget and the Problem of Scientific Change
    Kuhn's Model of Scientific Change   106
    Psychogenesis and the History of Science   108

6   Assessing Piaget's Conception of Evolution   125
    The Development of Piaget's Theory   126
    Problems with the Theory   130
    Constructive Evolution   138

    Notes   145
    Bibliography   155
    Index   161
    About the Author   167

Foreword

Piaget as a Philosopher

In many respects today's reader needs no introduction to the work and writings of Jean Piaget. His very attentive observations over many years of how children learn, often conducted in an experimental context of carefully contrived problems presented to children for their consideration and resolution, have become classic studies in the field of early cognitive psychology. Equally well known are his theoretical interpretations of these observational results, which he formulated into a general and complex model of an invariant series of stages and sub-stages through which the child's thought process develops. These issues have been extensively studied and evaluated by many later authors, whose overall accounts have thereby introduced the reader to Piaget's public persona. Although these topics are briefly discussed in Professor Messerly's book, they are not his primary concern. His focus lies elsewhere on another less familiar feature of Piaget's work which he himself has repeatedly said was of foundational, and of at least equal, importance for him.

Piaget tells us that in his private persona he was motivated throughout his career by the philosophical problem of relating biology to epistemology, i.e., determining how the relation between a living organism and its physical environment can be connected to the relation between the human mind and reality, or its epistemological environment. He was prepared for the former by his early academic training in biology, and for the latter by an equally early personal philosophical crisis precipitated by his disappointment with what he found in the writings of Henri Bergson.

Piaget's search for a link between biology and epistemology was his lifelong goal, and is the focus of Messerly's book. Thus what we find here is an account of Piaget's philosophical adventure, usually omitted in other studies of Piaget, which is quite worthy of study for its own intrinsic interest. Indeed, it is the fascinating story of how one of the most creative scientific minds of the twentieth century was constantly goaded by deeper philosophical questions, and how he gradually and patiently worked his way into a final, but highly controversial, resolution of these issues in his last years.

When Piaget is seen in this light, it becomes apparent, as he himself tells us, that his well-known studies of the genesis of intelligence in children were actually undertaken as a first attempt at building a bridge between biology and epistemology. Despite the immensity of observational detail and theoretical interpretation embodied in these studies, they played for him an instrumental role of becoming part of the superstructure of the bridge. The same can be said of his mid-career writings on the circle of the sciences, which attempt to draw developmental parallels between individual psychogenesis on the one hand and the history of thought, especially scientific thought, on the other. Piaget was well aware that the implied parallelism here between epistemological ontogenesis and phylogenesis was quite controversial, as also indeed was its original version in biology.

At a more fundamental level, Piaget gradually came to see that the mutual interactions found between the biological organism and its environment were also to be found in the relation between the mind and reality. He also saw that the basic unit of analysis in biology and psychology was not "static things with fixed properties," but rather dynamic processes and functions at both levels, which he then applied also to the epistemological problem. The net result was his discovery in all these cases of functions (self-regulatory organization, adaptation, assimilation, accommodation, and equilibration) which he became convinced were invariant. That insight is what ultimately held up the bridge between biology and epistemology, and thus turned out to be the object of his lifelong search.

He also carried the argument one step further. Since evolution is so basic to the organic world, it must also apply to the epistemological interactions between mind and reality. But which version of the theory of evolution fits both domains? Piaget had long been firmly committed to the dynamic conception of interactionism, i.e., that there is a two-way mutual exchange between organism/environment and mind/reality. As a result, he rejected both Darwinism (internal mutations tested later by external natural selection) and Lamarckianism (external changes resulting in the later internal inheritance of previously acquired characteristics.) From early on, Piaget had rejected both of these classical models of evolution as inconsistent with genuine interactionism. Late in his career he presented his own unique theory of evolution based on the idea of a "phenocopy," i.e., that external physical changes in the environment (new sensory experience in the case of epistemology) exert a non-specific influence on the genotype (on the rational mind in epistemology), moving it to act creatively to adapt to the new environment. Insofar as this theory does not see genetic mutations as fully random, it is not Darwinian. And insofar as this theory speaks of only an indeterminate message from the environment to the genotype, it is not Lamarckian. Piaget was quite aware that this theory of evolution was both unorthodox and quite bold. In his *Adaptation and Intelligence* (p.113) he even calls it a "hazardous hypothesis."

What are we to make of such a daring hypothesis? Piaget would surely tell us to treat it like any other scientific hypothesis. For what the scientist does is try to answer his fundamental problems by crafting comprehensive and reasonably explanatory hypotheses suggested by the data, and leave it to his own later work, or that of others, to try to verify or falsify it. This is precisely what has happened, and few have supported his hypothesis to date.

But evaluating that hypothesis is not the central point of this book. Rather what we have here primarily is a portrait of Piaget's life as a scientist which centers on his lifelong rethinking of the theory of evolution as the foundation of his entire project. It is a journey worth retaking with him because of its own intrinsic interest. It is an uncommon portrait of Piaget as a philosopher.

Richard J. Blackwell
Danforth Chair in Humanities
Saint Louis University

Preface

The entire career of one of the most significant intellectuals of the twentieth century was devoted to advancing a conception of evolution that applied to both biology and epistemology. Thus Piaget is best understood as an evolutionary epistemologist and biologist. Yet few scholars have taken note of this fact. While there are a plethora of books about Piaget's psychological and educational theories, there is no full-length study of Piaget as a philosopher and evolutionist. In fact, only a few works deal with Piaget's evolutionary and philosophical theories even tangentially.

This study attempts to fill that lacuna in scholarship. It is a sympathetic, developmental study of Piaget's conception of evolution. It treats his earliest formulations through his most sophisticated formulation as a constructivist theory of the evolution of human knowledge as continuous with, yet partially transcending, the biological process of adaptation to the environment. It begins with Piaget's first conjectures about knowledge and the subsequent study of the cognitive development in young children as an empirical check on an otherwise exclusively philosophical epistemology. It continues to trace Piaget's position as it develops in later studies, to its mature formulation as a "genetic epistemology" which extends the theory of the evolution of knowledge in individuals to that in the history of science. The work then turns to the promise of exploiting Piaget's evolutionary epistemology, especially in light of Piaget's distinctive theory of constructive evolution which is neither Darwinian nor Lamarckian. The advantage of this position is that it renders the evolutionary process as directional, rational, and progressive, thereby naturally leading to cognitive evolution.

I would like to thank the anonymous reader whose comments and suggestions were most helpful; Richard J. Blackwell, who introduced me to Piaget's thought, helped organize the project, and contributed greatly with the translations from the original French; my son, John Benjamin, whose computer expertise, emotional support and friendship were invaluable; and my wife, Jane, whose heart is full of warmth and love. May she not let the anguish of human life crush her gentle soul.

CHAPTER 1

Piaget's Problematic: The Parallels between Biology and Epistemology

Jean Piaget is universally recognized as one of the world's great child psychologists. He spent almost fifty years investigating how children learn, and these investigations have generated a voluminous amount of literature. For Piaget, these studies were merely the means he used to answer philosophical questions, which were his primary concern from the beginning. They provided part of the bridge between his two main interests: the nature of biological adaptation and epistemological questions concerning the nature and limits of human knowledge. He believed that the gap between biology and epistemology could be bridged by considering certain parallels between the two realms, the most significant of which is that both life and mind evolve. But in order to bridge the gap between biology and an analysis of knowledge, he needed a conception of evolution that was applicable to both. Thus, his theory of evolution served as a common explanatory device in both the biological and cognitive domains.

From the outset we note that Piaget's conception of evolution applies at various levels of reality and that the term "evolution" does not have a single application. At times it refers to the biological evolution of organisms, while at other times it refers to the development of psychological structures in children or the development of ideas in the history of science. To understand this puzzling shift between biological evolution, psychological development, and the history of science, it is necessary to understand the significance he attached to the regulative idea that "ontogeny recapitulates phylogeny."

Though interested from the beginning in reconstructing the evolution of human cognition, Piaget did not have direct access to the psychology of Neanderthal or the intellectual structures of Cro-Magnon. Thus, he was forced to invoke a method useful in biology—replacing phylogenesis with ontogenesis. In other words, the study of the growth of knowledge would focus on children rather than on primitive humans. We might say that the study of the development of cognitive structures in children was for Piaget a surrogate investigation. And, by invoking the idea that "ontogeny recapitulates phylogeny," he hoped to draw conclusions about the development of human knowledge that would be applicable to both individual cognitive development and to the growth of knowledge in the history of science. Furthermore, he hoped that the growth of knowledge would provide a model for biological evolution as well, since knowledge emerged from biology. Thus, it might be possible that one conception of evolution applied to all of these domains.

His inquiry led to all of the following questions: How do organisms evolve biologically? Are random mutations within the organism the catalyst for evolutionary change? How do children learn? Is learning a matter of trial and error and not in any way directed? How does science grow? Does it change through a series of incommensurable paradigm shifts or does it evolve in a progressive direction? Are there common or invariant laws which govern the transition between the various stages of development in biology, psychogenesis, and the history of science? Is there a common theory of evolution which accounts for the development of biological organisms, their cognitive processes, and scientific knowledge? Piaget's conception of evolution attempts to answer all of these questions.

We will trace Piaget's conception of evolution as it developed in a writing career that spanned more than seventy years. Chapter 1 considers the early biographical material that provides the context for the first formulation of his problematic, how to bridge the gap between biology and epistemology. We consider the parallels that can be drawn between life and mind which might close this gap. A clear delineation of the problematic sets the stage for his life's project—to respond to this problematic.

Chapter 2 investigates the early attempts to bridge the gap between life and mind. We are not concerned with analyzing the vast amount of empirical evidence accumulated during these years. Rather, we focus upon his first specific conception of the nature of the evolutionary process which is common to both biology and epistemology. This early conception of evolution derives primarily from the studies of individual psychogenetic development in children.

Chapter 3 turns our attention to Piaget's work on the epistemology of the sciences. We consider the nature of the evolutionary processes exhibited in mathematics, physics, and biology. Special emphasis will be placed upon the new science of "genetic epistemology," which investigates the growth of scientific knowledge, and the idea of "the circle of the sciences," which reveals the relationship between the sciences. In this chapter, the conception of evolution now incorporates evidence derived from the history of science and further specifies the evolutionary processes by which knowledge grows. Most importantly, the evidence allows for the extension of the evolutionary model from the intellectual development of children to the history of the sciences.

Chapter 4 focuses on the later writings concerning the relationship between biology and epistemology. These works represent his most mature thoughts concerning the parallels between biological and cognitive functioning and the processes by which they both evolve. They also effect a synthesis of his evolutionary thinking—Piaget's constructive evolution. The key idea in this synthesis is that behavior is the motor of a continual process of self-organization.

Chapter 5 applies this conception of evolution to the problem of scientific change. We investigate Piaget's most mature statement concerning the relationship between cognitive development in the individual and in the history of the sciences. He claimed that common mechanisms of evolutionary change are found in both psychogenesis and the history of science. Thus, we emphasize the applicability of the conception of evolution to problems in the philosophy of science. Piaget concluded that the growth of knowledge, both psychogenetic and in the history of science, is a constructive process.

Chapter 6 addresses selected problems with the theory: Can we extend the evolutionary analysis from biology to epistemology? Can we extend the model of evolution from psychogenesis to the history of the sciences? What reciprocal influence might the psychological and epistemological models have on a theory of biological evolution? In the final analysis, we reaffirm Piaget's major conclusion—the factual and empirical evidence give us reason to assert that evolution is a progressive, self-organizing, and constructive process.

The Formative Years

Piaget's Early Life

Jean Piaget was born on August 9, 1896 in Neuchâtel, Switzerland. His father was a historian who taught Piaget the value of systematic work and whom he greatly admired: "He is a man of painstaking and critical mind, who dislikes hastily improvised generalizations and who is not afraid to enter into a polemic when he saw historical truth deformed by respect for tradition."[1] His remarks concerning his mother were more reserved: "My mother was very intelligent, energetic, and fundamentally a very kind person; her rather neurotic temperament, however, made our family life somewhat troublesome."[2]

Piaget responded to this troubled family life by imitating his father and engaging in a private world of serious work. Between the ages of seven and ten, he was interested in mechanics, birds, fossils, and sea shells. At the age of ten, he wrote a one-page article on an albino sparrow which was published in a natural history journal! A short time later, he became an assistant to the director of the Natural History Museum in Neuchâtel. For four years, he worked as a naturalist in exchange for shells and mollusks that he added to his collection. When the director died in 1911, Piaget knew enough in this field to begin publishing on his own and was offered a position as curator of the mollusk collection at the Natural History Museum in Geneva. Piaget declined the offer because he was still in his early teens. However, he would later consider this experience as a naturalist crucial for his subsequent intellectual development, and for the preservation of his own psychological health throughout his adolescence. He wrote:

> These studies, premature as they were, were nevertheless of great value for my scientific development; moreover, they functioned if I may say so, as instruments of protection against the demon of philosophy. Thanks to them, I had the rare privilege of getting a glimpse of science and what it stands for before undergoing the philosophical crises of adolescence.[3]

Piaget's career as a naturalist was interrupted by a series of crises in his adolescence. First of all, there was the problem of religion. His mother had insisted that he take religious instruction, but his father believed that reason and faith were incompatible. Struck by the fact that much of religious dogma was irreconcilable with biology and that the arguments for the existence of God were surprisingly weak, he found consolation by reading Auguste Sabatier's *La philosophie de la religion fondee sur la psychologie et l'histoire*. The idea that religious dogmas were symbols which evolve was a much more satisfactory understanding of religious faith. A new passion—philosophy—now took hold of the young man.

Not surprisingly, his next crisis was philosophical. His godfather, Samuel Cornut, considered Piaget too specialized and introduced him to Bergson's *Creative Evolution*. Piaget recalled that this was the first time he had heard anyone who was not a theologian discuss philosophy. In his autobiography, he described his youthful encounter with Bergson:

> First of all, it was an emotional shock. I recall one evening of profound revelation. The identification of God with life itself was an idea that stirred me almost to ecstasy because it now enabled me to see in biology the explanation of all things and of the mind itself.

In the second place, it was an intellectual shock. The problem of knowing (properly called the epistemological problem) suddenly appeared to me in an entirely new perspective and as an absorbing topic of study. It made me decide to consecrate my life to the biological explanation of knowledge.[4]

But a closer examination of Bergson led to disappointment. He did not detect empirical rigor in Bergson; instead, he found an elaborate system without empirical evidence. This early encounter with Bergson had two effects upon him. First, it convinced him that knowledge must be explained biologically, and second, it persuaded him that philosophical speculation was not up to the task of reconciling the two. There was a conspicuous gap between biology and knowledge which needed to be closed by empirical study. Therefore the fundamental problem, which motivated Piaget's work and sustained his efforts for more than seventy years, was to find the means to close the gap between the biology and knowledge. But what was the connection between the two, between life and mind?

The First Ideas

About this time Piaget wrote "Sketch of a neo-pragmatism," an unpublished work in which he claimed that action admits of a kind of logic and that logic must stem from a sort of organization of our actions.[5] That is, as we organize our earliest experiences, we discover logical relationships. But this tentative attempt to explain logic, a specific kind of knowledge, had no connection with biology. What connection might there be between the two? The insight came from his university teacher, Arnold Reymond:

A lesson by A. Reymond on realism and nominalism within the problem area of "universals" (with some reference to the role of concepts in present-day science) gave me a sudden insight. I had thought deeply on the problem of "species" in zoology and had adopted an entirely nominalistic point of view in this respect. The "species" has no reality in itself and is distinguished from the simple "varieties" merely by a greater stability. But this theoretical view, inspired by Lamarckism, bothered me somewhat in my empirical work (viz. classification of mollusks). The dispute of Durkheim and Tarde on reality or non-reality of society as an organized whole plunged me into a similar state of uncertainty without making me see, at first, its pertinence to the problem of the species. Aside from this the general problem of realism and of nominalism provided me with an over-all view: I suddenly understood that at all levels (viz. that of the living cell, organism, species, society, etc.) but also with reference to the states of conscience, to concepts, to logical principles, etc. one finds the same problem of the relationship between the parts and the whole; hence I was convinced that I had found the solution. There at last was the close union that I had dreamed of between biology and philosophy, there was an access to an epistemology which to me then seemed really scientific![6]

In this passage, Piaget began to see a possible parallel between biology and knowledge. The problem of universals (a logical and philosophical problem) parallels the problem of species (a biological problem). The relationship of part and whole is operative at both of these levels and at all other levels of reality. For instance, an individual member of a biological species is made of component parts and at the same time that individual is a part of the species. Might epistemology be made scientific by using the part as a model for the whole? Perhaps this part/whole parallel might close the gap between biology and knowledge.

But why does the part/whole parallel in the biological and cognitive domains provide an access to a scientific epistemology? Because Piaget was aware that the individual organism (a part of the species) is used as a model for understanding the species (the whole) in biology under the regulative idea that "ontogeny recapitulates phylogeny." In biology the ontogenesis of the individual provides a model for the phylogenesis of the species. He began to believe that the emergence of knowledge in the individual (the part) would provide a model for the emergence of knowledge in the human species (the whole). In effect, one could study epistemological questions concerning the growth of knowledge, specifically scientific knowledge, by studying the growth of knowledge in children. This parallel between biology and knowledge was part of the bridge that he needed.

Next, he completed another unpublished work, "On Realism and Nominalism in the Life-Sciences." Here, for the first time, he suggested that "totalities" or wholes exist which are qualitatively distinct from their parts, repudiating the nominalism he had embraced earlier regarding species. These organic, mental, and social wholes impose organization on their parts. The interaction of whole and parts varies from structure to structure, but reciprocal preservation of the parts and whole provides the most stable equilibrium for the structure. In this work, Piaget also introduced the idea of equilibrium, a balance of the opposing tendencies of parts and wholes, in what he later would call a "total structure" (*structure totale*). Piaget was surprised to find that much of his theorizing concerning totalities had been anticipated by Aristotle, since Aristotle's concept of form is a "totality" imposing organization on the biological species. What Piaget saw was that a naturalistic—i.e., not transcendental or supernatural—explanation of mind was possible and that Bergson's dualism between the vital and logical may be unnecessary.

At this point, he continued to pursue doctorates in both philosophy and biology and contemplated developing a general theory of knowledge from a biological point of view. Still, he needed to decide if this project entailed several semesters' work in psychology to provide the empirical evidence deemed necessary. While finishing his doctorate in biology, he spent some time in the mountains in order to make a decision. What he wrote during this period was a philosophical novel entitled *Recherche*, in which many of his seminal ideas were contained.

The First Writings

In the novel, the central character discovered that the idea of species serves as the starting point for any serious discussion of biology, morality, sociology, aesthetics and even religion. Evolution was contained in the study of species, morality grew from the relationship between individuals and species, as did social institutions, aesthetics and religion. Furthermore all of reality, and the sciences that study it, can be understood in terms of the relationship between parts and whole. Though organization is an equilibrium between the whole and the parts, it is an unstable equilibrium because of the interference of other systems and the organism's tendency toward ideal organization. Ideal organization is an ideal equilibrium toward which all things tend by the very fact of their existence. Still this tendency does not imply finality, only that laws govern the process that leads toward ideal equilibrium. Science provides the means of understanding ideal organization because it reveals that laws govern the tendency toward organization.

What kinds of laws did Piaget believe govern the process by which organisms tend toward ideal equilibrium? He claimed that four laws govern organic equilibrium. First, organization tends to preserve itself. This results when the qualities of the whole and parts are compatible. Second, the environment tends to disrupt this equilibrium, and the parts and wholes fight for survival with each other. Third, the parts and wholes modify each other when each tries to preserve itself. Finally, all forms of equilibrium tend toward the first law, preservation and reciprocity between part and whole. The first law denotes an ideal equilibrium since all real equilibria tend toward it, and it is the only stable equilibrium.

Piaget's discussion of ideal equilibrium in *Recherche* provided a glimpse of his earliest conception of the evolutionary process. Evolution progresses toward a stable equilibrium between the individual and species. Nevertheless, there are no final causes governing this process, and it is not teleological because equilibrium "is a result and not a goal."[7]

Note the comparisons that can be made between his earliest conception of evolution and some of the seminal ideas of ancient Greeks. While Piaget's conception of ideal equilibrium is not a developmental Platonism, since this ideal does not exist independently of its contents, it is close to Aristotle's concept of form as the organizational tendency or structure of a thing. A major difference between the two is that Piaget's evolution toward ideal equilibrium is not teleological. For Piaget, the outcome emerges through the continual interaction of organism and environment—rather than being determined in advance—and the organism's interaction with the environment introduces novelty. Another difference between Piaget and Aristotle is that ideal equilibrium may change given the influence of external factors, contrasting dramatically with Aristotle's conception of forms. We might think of Piaget's early notion of evolution as a non-teleological Aristotelianism.

Piaget's other early writings stressed the importance of evolution. In a prose poem entitled "La mission de l'idée," he identified the evolutionary process with the Good and argued that evolution brings life, harmony, and unity. And, in a short article entitled "Biology and War," he discussed the relationship between heredity and environment and the mechanisms of evolutionary adaptation. This was the first time he stated that neither Darwinism nor Lamarckism adequately explains evolution, a notion that would play a major role in his subsequent theorizing.

Major Influences

The Influence of Bergson

We have already noted the influence of Bergson on Piaget. In *Recherche* the importance of the concept of genera is traced to Bergson. In addition, Piaget's idea that cognition derives from action, not language, can be found in Bergson. Most importantly for our purposes, one finds in Bergson arguments for a biological theory of knowledge.

> Theory of knowledge and theory of life seem to us inseparable . . .
> a theory of knowledge which does not replace the intellect in the
> general evolution of life will teach us neither how the frames of
> knowledge have been constructed nor how we can enlarge or go
> beyond them. It is necessary that these two inquires, theory of
> knowledge and theory of life, should join each other, and, by a
> circular process, push each other on unceasingly.[8]

In fact, Bergson opened *Creative Evolution* by claiming that intelligence is an evolutionary adaption.

The history of the evolution of life shows us in the faculty of understanding an appendage of the faculty of acting, a more and more precise, more and more complex and supple adaptation of the consciousness of living beings to the conditions of existence that are made for them. Hence should result this consequence that our intellect, in the narrow sense of the word, is intended to secure the perfect fitting of our body to its environment, to represent the relations of external things among themselves.[9]

Bergson rejected both a mechanistic and a finalistic interpretation of evolution. A mechanistic interpretation cannot do justice to the development of complex forms in evolution. The development of greater degrees of complexity involves risk and if survival value were the only factor in evolution, then it would cease with simple organisms. The effective functioning of the whole cannot be attributed to chance. This is incredulous! But an explanation in terms of finality will not do either. This would mean that evolution is determined and that novelty and creativity would be eliminated. There must then be an immanent teleology at work in the organism, though this is not the progressive realization of a preconceived plan.

In order to explain the process of evolution, Bergson argued for a vital impulse (*elan vital*) as an alternative to finalism and mechanism. One of the reasons Bergson posited the "*elan vital*" was because of his sharp distinction between intuition and intelligence. The intellect has as its object what is discontinuous and stable; it treats the living in the same way as the non-living by reducing the living to its constituent parts. The intellect cannot comprehend life's continuity and duration, and it spatializes time by taking static pictures of a continuous process, not allowing for the continual creation which it understands mechanistically or finalistically. What faculty can grasp the vital impulse which creates through matter? Since the intellect cannot grasp movement, it must be some other faculty. Instinct is closer to life but it cannot reflect and, if it could, it would reflect upon the vital. The faculty which can reflect upon the vital is intuition, which is "instinct that has become disinterested, self-conscious, capable of reflecting on its object and of enlarging it indefinitely."[10] Reflective consciousness is split into intelligence, which corresponds to matter, and intuition, which corresponds to life.

It is here that some differences between Bergson and Piaget emerge. In the first place, according to Piaget, Bergson's theoretical speculations on the relation of mind and biology needed an experimental link. Bergson too quickly assumed that science cannot understand life because it must reduce life to the sum of its parts. Piaget, on the other hand, believed that a general scientific theory of the structure of the whole is possible. Secondly, he did not accept Bergson's split between intuition and intelligence because, as we will see, Piaget was hostile to intuition as a method. Finally, he completely rejected the irrationalism in Bergson, since Piaget believed there is a logic to action. A logic of action and a theory of structures result in a dynamic and rationalist account of structures. Piaget rejected mechanistic, finalistic, and vitalistic accounts of evolution and was committed to a naturalistic account of evolution and its processes. But despite the many differences between the two thinkers there can be little doubt that Piaget shared Bergson's overall view of philosophy, particularly the belief that evolution plays a significant role in the naturalistic explanation of knowledge. His conception of evolution was directly influenced by Bergson, and he meant his theory of evolution to overcome the deficiencies he found in Bergson.

The Influence of Spencer

In his youth, Bergson was a devotee of Spencer and his *Creative Evolution* was written with Spencer as a point of departure. Spencer, like Bergson and Piaget, was first and foremost an evolutionary thinker who accorded evolution a central place in his naturalistic explanation of knowledge. But Spencer's conception of evolution was mechanistic, not vitalistic like Bergson's. Spencer's formula of evolution runs thus:

> Evolution is an integration of matter and a concomitant dissipation of motion; during which the matter passes from an indefinite,

incoherent homogeneity to a definite, coherent heterogeneity; and during which the retained motion undergoes a parallel trans-formation.[11]

According to Spencer, whether we consider the formation of planets out of the nebular mass, of complex organisms from simple ones, complex societies from primeval ones, or science and philosophy from sensations and perceptions, evolution moves from the relatively indefinite to the relatively definite, from incoherence to coherence. This evolution is accompanied by a progressive differentiation from the homogeneous to the heterogeneous, but all this motion eventually comes to rest as it meets resistance. The integration of matter is accompanied by a dissipation of motion; hence the process of evolution tends toward an equilibrium, a balance of forces, which is succeeded by dissolution and disintegration. Moreover, the processes of evolution and dissolution will repeat endlessly.

A salient point of Spencer's evolutionary thinking is the concept of equilibration, the balancing of forces. Piaget found his idea of equilibration in the philosophy of Spencer. Spencer, like Piaget, extended evolutionary theory into various domains. The most important similarities between Spencer and Piaget are the central explanatory role they found for evolution and the attempt both made to articulate a naturalistic theory of knowledge to close the gap between life and mind.

Nevertheless, there are significant differences between their evolutionary theories. First, Spencer interpreted the Lamarckian theory of inheritance literally, whereas Piaget rejected a pure Lamarckism. Second, Spencer was an empiricist who believed the growth of knowledge is an additive and accumulative process, whereas Piaget explicitly rejected this view. Third, Spencer's conviction that reason is innate and largely immutable directly contrasts with Piaget's belief that the evolution of reason continues in science. Finally, and most importantly, Piaget's experimentalism had no counterpart in Spencer. Piaget asked questions with empirical content and equilibrium was, in his mind, an exclusively biological phenomenon.

Historico-Critical Philosophy of Science

Another influence upon Piaget's thought was a movement in France known as "historico-critical philosophy of science."[12] The key individuals in the movement included Piaget's teacher Arnold Reymond, Leon Brunschvicg, Henri Poincaré, Alexander Koyré, and Emile Meyerson among others. All of these thinkers were concerned with an analysis of the basic concepts underlying scientific knowledge. In this endeavor they were strongly influenced by Kant, as was Piaget himself, and as a group they constituted a type of Neo-Kantianism.

These thinkers rejected Kant's transcendental deduction of the categories, and looked to the "historical" development of reason in the history of science. There could be no Kantian transcendental deduction because the categories of thought change over time. The group endorsed a kind of historicism, i.e., the idea that understanding a concept depends upon an investigation of its origin and development. Piaget agreed with the historico-critical thinkers that the study of the history of science is a study or critique of the evolution of human reason, and his work in psychogenesis carried out this program on the individual level. Both the ontogeny and the phylogeny of reason attempt to understand the "evolution of reason."

Meyerson's influence upon Piaget was of particular importance. Meyerson's search for the basic principles of human knowledge led him to postulate two such principles, the law of legality and the law of causality.[13] Both of these principles govern human's interpretation of nature and both require that nature conform to law. The desire for conformity between nature and law manifests itself in the laws of science, as well as in the common sense belief that permanent substance underlies change. The tendency to bring nature into conformity with law reveals itself in the law of identity, which is the most fundamental law of the human mind. (Examples of this law: $A = A$; $F = ma$; $E = mc^2$.) The law of identity asserts permanence but cannot account for a change and leads us to a Parmenidean universe—one eternally immutable.

Bergson resolved this issue with a dualistic theory of knowledge in which science deals with the permanent and intuition with the changing. Piaget saw that if he wanted to avoid this dualism he had to reconcile logic, manifested in the law of identity, with change and process. Piaget, we might remember, had argued that logic arises from action and that logical principles like the law of identity are not innate but develop through time. Piaget sought to reconcile the development of knowledge through time with the certainty that knowledge provides because a theory of knowledge must account for the development of knowledge without collapsing into a relativism. His problematic was clearly taking shape; he must close the gap between biological life, which exhibits itself as continuously changing, and scientific knowledge, which bases itself on immutable principles. Perhaps part of this bridge might be provided by the theory of biological evolution. But can this theory account for the growth of knowledge in the individual and scientific knowledge as well?

We might also remember Piaget's intellectual milieu—the late nineteenth and early twentieth century. Piaget was basically a nineteenth-century thinker. The characteristic feature of the nineteenth century was its historical or evolutionary perspective, and the leading intellectuals of the day, almost without exception, were evolutionary thinkers. In addition to Bergson and Spencer, Hegel, Marx, Comte, and Freud all adopted evolutionary perspectives. Hegel built an entire philosophy around the evolution of Absolute Spirit; Marx's philosophy concerned itself with social, historical, and economic evolution; Comte's laws of the stages of religion, metaphysics, and science were evolutionary; and Freud's psychological theorizing was developmental or evolutionary. No doubt Bergson and Spencer, the more biologically oriented evolutionists, had the greatest influence on Piaget. But almost all nineteenth-century thinkers shared a belief that life evolves according to laws and that evolution moves in a specific direction.

Note also how the nature of logic and reason for these nineteenth-century thinkers was quite different from the notion we find in Kant, Descartes, or Plato. Reason was no longer pure, static, and contemplative; it evolved. But what, if anything, remained stable throughout the process of the evolution of reason? Are there any invariant principles governing cognitive organization? Piaget needed to reconcile these fundamental and immutable processes—if any exist—with the nature of biological change in order to advance a biologically based theory of knowledge.

The Connection between Philosophy and Science

But why was Piaget so interested in a "scientific" rather than a "speculative" epistemology? And why must his epistemological theorizing be informed by a scientific theory like evolution? To answer these questions, one need only recall Piaget's intellectual background. He remembered his early experiences with Bergson, Spencer, and Reymond, and he regarded speculation uninformed by science as intellectually dishonest. Speculation, based upon intuition, is not justified in making claims about facts. He clearly expressed his attitude toward speculative thinking:

> It was while teaching philosophy that I saw how easily one can say ... what one wants to say .... In fact, I became particularly aware of the dangers of speculation, which attracted me. It's a natural tendency. It's so much easier than digging out facts. You sit in your office and build a system. It's wonderful. But with my training in biology, I felt this kind of undertaking was precarious.[14]

Philosophical speculation can raise questions, but it cannot provide the answers that are found only in testing and experimentation. For instance, any supposed relationship between biology and knowledge must be demonstrated inasmuch as knowledge presupposes verification, and verification is attained by mutually agreed upon controls. Unfortunately, philosophers do not usually have experience in inductive and experimental verification.

> Young philosophers because they are made to specialize immediately on entering the university in a discipline which the greatest thinkers in the history of philosophy have entered only after years of scientific investigations, believe they have immediate access to

the highest regions of knowledge, when neither they nor sometimes their teachers have the least experience of what it is to acquire and verify a specific piece of knowledge.[15]

Philosophers employ the method of reflection, which is based upon intuition. The deficiencies of this method had become apparent to him in the philosophies of Bergson and Spencer, who made claims regarding the realm of facts based upon their own reflection. But the only justifiable methods with which to make claims about the facts are the experimental and inductive method. Reflection, based upon intuition, cannot give us information in the realm of facts. But how did the method of philosophy become separate from the scientific method? Traditionally philosophy associated itself closely with science and its methods; the two were virtually indistinguishable. But, beginning in the nineteenth century, philosophy came to believe itself capable of a "suprascientific" knowledge. This split was disastrous for philosophy because it retreated to its own world, and its credibility became questioned. For Piaget, traditional philosophy is synonymous with science or reflections upon science. In this sense, his own reflection on evolutionary theory constituted traditional philosophizing, and he had always maintained that philosophical reflection uninformed by science cannot arrive at truth—it can only provide subjective wisdom. His life's work attempts to inform philosophical speculation with empirical evidence.

Piaget's Problematic

Since Piaget tried to interpret knowledge biologically, he invoked explanations of organic reality to explain cognition. But why should we be able to apply biological theories to cognition? Because in both areas analogies exist which invite the use of the same explanatory principles, including a theory of evolution. Furthermore, the fact that mind is an expression of life provides an adequate reason for supposing a relationship exists between life and mind. Piaget saw the way to a scientific epistemology—a possible way to bridge the gap between biology and knowledge—through the parallels between the two, especially in a theory of evolution that would be applicable to both. But he did not presuppose that an evolutionary parallel existed between life and mind and this parallelism could not be established until after the evidence for the biological nature of human cognition had been presented.

Piaget envisioned an evolutionary theory which could be applied to biology, psychology, and epistemology. The problem was to show why this might be the case, i.e., why evolution has such vast explanatory powers. It must explain the occurrence of both biological organisms and of thought in the universe, particularly scientific thought. Beginning as a young biologist dedicated to analyzing human knowledge, he set out to unify biology and epistemology.

It might be objected that we are misconstruing Piaget's problematic, since an alternative view is that Piaget's problematic was the reconciliation of science and values.[16] We maintain that Piaget gave up—or at least radically reinterpreted—this project. Disappointed that Bergson had failed to provide any empirical basis for his evolutionary philosophy, he recognized the need for psychology as the empirical pursuit which would help bridge his gap. He saw the possibility of an empirically and biologically based epistemology and pursued this project throughout his lifetime.

Nevertheless, it is true that Piaget's religious writings pursued the science-value problematic.[17] But these writings were early in his career and he never returned to them, indicating that they were not his primary concern. Yet he regularly returned to the issue of the connection between life and mind, and his entire opus is the legacy of this attempt to articulate a biological theory of knowledge. Without his early scientific training, he may have pursued the more metaphysical questions. But there is much evidence to suggest that he did not consider metaphysical speculation about the relationship of science and values to be valuable.[18]

There can be little doubt that scientific knowledge, specifically about the relationship of biology and epistemology, provided the answer for Piaget's problem. In the Foreword to *The Essential Piaget*, he confirmed that the relationship between biology and epistemology provided the context for his work.

The authors of this anthology have understood perfectly . . . that my efforts directed toward the psychogenesis of knowledge were for me only a link between two dominant preoccupations; the search for the mechanisms of biological adaptation and the analysis of that higher form of adaptation which is scientific thought, the epistemological interpretation of which has always been my central aim.[19]

While the most important part of Piaget's solution to his problematic was a conception of evolution, some of the other parallels between biology and epistemology were also significant. First, both are concerned with the problem of parts and wholes. In biology the study of development of individual members of the species (the ontogenesis of the parts) provides clues to the development of the species as a whole (the phylogenesis of the whole). In an analogous manner, the development of the individual's knowledge (psychogenesis) provides clues to the development of the knowledge attained by the group (scientific knowledge). Second, in both realms there exist organized totalities which manifest themselves as structures, whether biological or cognitive. Third, both biological and cognitive systems adapt to the environment. This manifests itself in the biological relationship of organism and environment and in the cognitive relationship between subjective knowers and the object of their knowledge. Finally, and most importantly, both cognitive and biological structures evolve rationally according to laws. Evolution is a significant part of the parallel between biological and cognitive systems and the thread that weaves throughout Piaget's thought.

That Piaget is to be understood as an evolutionary thinker is beyond doubt, as recent scholarship reveals. Michael Chapman maintains that "his particular conception of constructive evolution allies him with other thinkers who have sought meaning in human life in the process of evolutionary change."[20] And Richard Kitchener asserts:

There can be little doubt that Piaget's basic philosophical orientation is evolutionary. If there is a single leitmotif in Piaget's thinking it is this: All reality—biological, physical, psychological, socio-logical, intellectual—is evolving in the direction of progress.[21]

In the next chapter we will consider the development of cognitive structures in the individual (psychogenesis). Piaget undertook these investigations as a way of beginning to bridge his gap, hoping that this inquiry would provide clues to the laws which govern evolutionary development.

> While I wanted to devote myself to biology, I had an equal interest in the problems of objective knowledge and in epistemology. My decision to study the development of the cognitive functions in the child was related to my desire to satisfy the two interests in one activity. By considering development as a kind of mental embryo-genesis, one could construct a biological theory of knowledge.[22]

A biological theory of knowledge would allow him to extend his evolutionary analysis from biology to psychology. More importantly, the studies of children provided the opportunity to formulate his first specific conception of the nature of the process of evolution which is common to both biology and epistemology.

CHAPTER 2

The Early Assessment of Evolution: The Study of Psychogenesis

Piaget left for Zurich in 1918 shortly after receiving his doctorate in biology with the aim of beginning his psychological investigations. His purpose was to find a situation conducive to the aim of gathering empirical evidence about the growth of human knowledge that might be consistent with his biological training. Unable to find such a situation in Zurich, he went to Paris the following autumn and spent two years at the Sorbonne. He attended the lectures of L. Brunschvicg, whose classes exerted a lasting influence on him with their emphasis on psychology and the historico-critical method. During this time Piaget had the good fortune to encounter Dr. Theophile Simon, who had Binet's laboratory at his disposal. Simon invited Piaget to standardize tests on Parisian children, marking his introduction to child psychology.

While evaluating children's intelligence tests, Piaget became interested in the reasons children fail to answer questions correctly. By engaging them in conversation, he sought to uncover the reasoning processes that underlie their incorrect responses. He noticed that simple reasoning concerning parts and whole was very difficult for children up to the age of eleven or twelve, suggesting that older children are qualitatively different from younger ones in their intellectual development. He continued to analyze the verbal reasoning of children by questioning them regarding part-whole and cause-effect relationships. He enthusiastically described his good fortune in discovering a method to test some of his theoretical ideas.

> At last I had found my field of research. First of all it became clear to me that the theory of the relations between the whole and the part can be studied experimentally through analysis of the psychological processes underlying logical operations. This marked the end of my "theoretical" period and the start of an inductive and experimental era in the psychological domain which I always had wanted to enter, but for which until then I had not found the suitable problems. Thus my observations that logic is not inborn, but develops little by little, appeared to be consistent with my ideas on the formation of the equilibrium toward which the evolution of mental structures tends; moreover, the possibility of directly studying the problem of logic was in accord with all my former philosophical interests. Finally, my aim of discovering a sort of embryology of intelligence fit in with my biological training; from the start of my theoretical thinking I was certain that the problem of the relation between the organism and environment extended also into the realm of knowledge, appearing here as the problem of the relation between the acting or thinking subject and the objects of his experience. Now I had the chance of studying this problem in terms of psychogenetic development.[1]

Piaget's earliest empirical observations would prove consistent with his theoretical speculations. Logical thinking develops over time and is an equilibrium which is gradually attained. Thus mental embryogenesis parallels physical genesis, and the study of the development of cognitive structures provided the bridge between his biological and epistemological interests. These studies would answer epistemological questions about how knowledge is attained from a biological or developmental point of view. There is little doubt that he already believed that the study of psychogenetic development would shed light upon epistemological puzzles. In addition, the relationship between thinking subject and the objects of their knowledge parallels a biological relationship between organism and environment. He intended to spend only a few years on this project and then apply his observations to epistemological questions. But, as it turned out, several decades were necessary for the investigations.

The Study of Children's Thinking

The Early Research

In 1921 Piaget was offered a position as director of research at the Jean-Jacques Rousseau Institute of Geneva. The research he conducted there during the next four years formed the basis for his first five books in child psychology and was reported therein.[2] Still, they provide an early glimpse of his ideas concerning the evolution of cognitive structures.

Piaget's first work, *The Language and Thought of the Child* (1923), described, not surprisingly, the development of language and thought in the child. He observed that a substantial part of children's speech was egocentric until the age of seven or eight and that socialized speech became more prominent thereafter. The detailed observations upon which this conclusion was based need not concern us. Most important for our purposes is the fact that his earliest observations demonstrated that language and thought evolve. The view that the language and thought of the human subject evolve over time exemplifies Piaget's basic philosophical orientation.

In the conclusion of *The Language and Thought of the Child*, Piaget turned to the functional aspects of language and thought and quotes the eminent psychologist E. Claparède extensively. Claparède believed that children become aware of categories of thought (cause, effect, aims, place) when their previous explanations are non-adaptive. The need for a better explanation forces reflection which eventually creates consciousness of the categories. Because children are not perfectly adapted, they ask questions and become conscious of categories, whereas completely instinctual creatures—being well-adapted—have no need to ask questions. Piaget agreed with Claparède.

> The study of categories is . . . a study of functional psychol-
> ogy . . . Here the psychologist meets on common ground with the
> historian of science and the modern logician. Traditional logic,
> whether we take the realism of the Schools or Kant's apriorism,
> regarded the categories as fixed, and imposed on the mind and on
> things once and for all, and in a definite form. This hypothesis is
> psychologically false . . . From this angle the problem of categories
> must therefore be formulated in connection with the intellectual
> development of the child himself. The genetician will therefore
> have to note the appearance and use of these categories at every
> stage of intelligence traversed by the child, and to bring these facts
> under the functional laws of thought.[3]

If logic is not innate, it develops. This development should interest the psychologist, logician, and historian of science who study the development of these categories in the history of science. Observing development will determine how knowledge comes to be. Piaget was already aware that the development of the organism must be explained in terms of "functional laws of thought" which govern cognitive evolution from one stage to another.

The basic conclusion of this work is that the evolution of thought proceeds from a knowledge of the physical world, to the development of formal categories to describe it, and, finally, to the development of formal categories that apply to names, classifications, definitions, judgments, i.e., logical justification. Some as yet unspecified need drives this "governed-by-functional-processes" evolution. At this point in his career, Piaget did not articulate definitive conception of the evolutionary/developmental process that is applicable to cognition, but the empirical evidence suggested that the developing intellect needed an evolutionary explanation. At least two questions were developing in his mind. Is intellectual evolution governed by laws, and does it proceed in a certain direction?

His next book, *Judgment and Reasoning in the Child* (1924), continued these investigations. It concentrated on the development of logical reasoning in the child, especially Piaget's fascination with the contradictions characteristic of children's thought. He had discovered that until at least the age of seven or eight, the child has no sense of contradiction. How then do we explain the gradual elimination of contradictory thinking in children in psychological terms? Why does the mind become more logical as it matures?

> Non-contradiction is a state of equilibrium in contrast to the state of permanent disequilibrium which is the normal life of the mind. For, as every one knows nowadays, sensations, images, pleasure and pain, in short all the "immediate data of consciousness" are born along on a continuous "stream of consciousness." Exactly the same thing applies to the immediate data of the external world; they constitute Heraclitus' eternal becoming. A certain number of fixed points stand out in contrast to this flux, such as concepts and the relations subsisting between them, in a word, the whole universe of logic, which in the very process of its formation is independent of time and consequently in a state of equilibrium.[4]

The psychological equivalent of non-contradiction is equilibrium. The evolution of mind from contradiction to non-contradiction is an advance toward a psychological equilibrium. The concept of equilibrium will play a central role in Piaget's mature conception of how the process of evolution moves along and is especially important because it reveals one of the most important ways biology and cognition are linked: both advance toward equilibrium. He did not yet offer a theory of equilibration, but he did suggest that the mind moves unceasingly toward it. At this point, equilibrium was characterized as the reversibility of psychological operations.[5] The recognition that equilibrium is as much a process as a state is a manifestation of his basic evolutionary approach.

Piaget's first two books had reported the empirical evidence that supported his earliest reflections concerning the evolutionary process. This evidence was crucial in order to avoid a speculative epistemology. The most important ideas he derived from these investigations were that: 1) language, thought, judgment, and reasoning of the child evolve; 2) processes of this evolution are governed by laws or mechanisms; 3) logical thinking develops by reflecting upon actions; and 4) higher forms of knowledge are characterized by equilibrium.

Intellectual Evolution

The Child's Conception of the World (1926) detailed the tendency of children to think about the world from various perspectives. Children think about the world as: realists—who attribute objective reality to subjective phenomena; animists—who attribute animate properties to inanimate things; and artificialists—who attribute intentionality and finality to natural phenomena. Piaget found that these tendencies gradually diminish as children and their conception of the world evolve. We can imagine him wondering if scientific thought evolved along similar lines or if he could uncover the mechanisms of this gradual evolution.

His next work, *The Child's Conception of Physical Causality* (1927), described the child's understanding of the causes of natural phenomena like the origin of wind, the movement of clouds, stars, and rivers, the displacement of water, and the idea of force. He found that the concept of causality, like logic and language, evolves systematically through a series of stages.[6] Successive stages reach increasingly accurate and complex explanations of physical causality. At the end of this work, Piaget summarized the views contained in it, as well as those in *The Child's Conception of the World*. He concluded that intellectual development goes through a number of distinct stages. At each stage the mind believes that it apprehends reality as it is—that it knows the truth—even though the content of each stage differs dramatically when one considers a young child or a mature scientist.

While the scientist and child view reality differently, they both try to establish harmony with the perceived reality. But how might we compare various stages of intellectual development to determine which is more advanced? Piaget suggested that we can consider them from one of two points of view. We can accept science as the conventional standard because scientific knowledge developed later than children's. On this view, though scientific knowledge is not absolute, it can serve as a criterion for assessing the development of knowledge in children. Granting scientific knowledge as a norm, the development of knowledge in children can be studied by psychology, since psychological norms provide developmental standards. The other alternative regards neither system of reference as normative, and no claim is made concerning which perspective more closely corresponds to reality. Such an approach lends itself to epistemological speculation concerning the relationship between mind and reality. Piaget made it clear that he followed the first approach. If, on the one hand, we accept that scientific knowledge is more adequate than children's knowledge, then the study of how children come to achieve scientific knowledge is amenable to an evolutionary explanation. If, on the other hand, we assume no connection between mind and reality or assume that all theories concerning the nature of reality are relative, then it is obvious that epistemology must remain speculative. Piaget favored the former approach.

In this work he also enunciated his view on the relationship between mind and reality. A central question for epistemology is whether the organism is molded by its environment—empiricism—by its stable internal structures—a priorism—or by an interaction between the two. It was this third option that he found most appealing, since it allows for the adaptation of thought to reality as evolutionary transformation proceeds. Here we see the foreshadowing of a number of Piaget's basic ideas: 1) that intelligence is an extension of organic functioning; 2) that the relationship of thought to things parallels the relationship of organism to environment; and, 3) that theories concerning this relationship apply to epistemology and biology. Here Piaget claimed that words like empiricism and apriorism have only a psychological and not an epistemological meaning. Yet he maintained that the results of these investigations into psychogenesis might be extended to intellectual evolution as a whole. How might this be accomplished? While we cannot assume stage B is better than stage A, since we do not have any standard to which both can be compared, we can determine how stages A, B, C, . . . and Z relate to each other. Whatever conclusions we reach about these relationships—say that stage C does something that B does not do—may be profitably generalized as characteristic of the whole series. Thus the relationship between stages at various levels of development provides the key to understanding the growth processes of the stages. And it may be that the "fragmentary" conclusions reached by the analysis of stages provides clues to a "general" conclusion concerning the process.

> To put things more concretely, it may very well be that the psychological laws arrived at by means of our restricted method can be extended into epistemological laws arrived at by the analysis of the history of the sciences: the elimination of realism, of substantialism, of dynamism, the growth of relativism, etc., all these are evolutionary laws which appear to be common both to the development of the child and to that of scientific thought.[7]

The evolutionary laws which govern the transition from one stage of cognitive development to another may be generalized into epistemological laws. One can easily imagine that these evolutionary laws explain ethical, political, and social evolution as well. Still, Piaget was tentative about extending his findings regarding psychological development to other areas.

> We are in no way suggesting, it need hardly be said, that our psychological results will admit straight away of being generalized into epistemological laws. All we expect is that with the cooperation of methods more powerful than our own (historical, sociological methods, etc.), it will be possible to establish between our conclusions and those of epistemological analysis a relation of particular case to general law, or rather of infinitesimal variation to the whole of the curve.[8]

Piaget's remarks reveal his own uncertainty regarding the generalization of his limited conclusions. He appears to waver on the issue, at times remaining quite tentative, at other times asserting the connection between his limited psychological findings and biological and epistemological issues. As his career progressed, he became more confident about generalizing the results of his psychological investigations.

The remainder of *The Child's Conception of Physical Causality* interpreted the evolution of the child's notions of reality, causality, and law. Piaget noted the important contribution of both mind and environment in intellectual evolution. He also referred to the concepts of imitation—the organism's adapting to the environment by reproducing or representing external events or phenomena, and assimilation—the incorporation of the new into the pre-existing structure. The idea of imitation clearly foreshadows his later notion of assimilation. Piaget suggested at the end of the work that when these two tendencies are antagonistic, an unstable equilibrium results.

While Piaget formulated these ideas more precisely as his own thought matured, these early studies exerted a profound influence upon him. Some of the ideas informed by this early research which are relevant to his view of evolution include: 1) that the growth of knowledge in children originates from the interaction between organism and environment; 2) that this process leads to a more adequate and stable relationship between the two; and 3) that understanding this process may shed light on epistemological problems. In other words, the evolutionary/developmental character of intellectual development has both biological and epistemological implications.

A Biological Theory of Knowledge

The Biological Research

After conducting his early research, Piaget assumed the chair in philosophy at the University of Neuchâtel in 1925, succeeding his former teacher A. Reymond. Piaget spent much of his time teaching philosophy of science and developing an expertise in the history of science, endeavors which served him well in the comparisons he would later make between the history of science and childhood development. Finally, he was kept busy by the birth of his three children, and his observations of them would provide the material for his next three books.[9]

During this time he also conducted biological research on mollusks, the subject of his doctoral dissertation.[10] This research pertained to the influence of heredity and environment on morphogenesis. The problem exists not only in biology but in learning theory and epistemology as well. He was aware of a snail, *Limnaea stagnalis*, which had an elongated shell in tranquil waters. In the great lakes of Switzerland where the waters are turbulent, the snail has a globular shape which can be explained as a phenotypic adaptation to the action of the waves which force the snails to clamp themselves to the shore. By observing 80,000 individuals, Piaget found that the snails globular shape became hereditarily fixed. Not only did they not revert to the elongated shape when bred in still waters, but a pure species could be bred according to the Mendelian laws of cross breeding. He concluded that these findings were not easily explained according to the Darwinian principles of random mutation and natural selection because the mutations were not random, and the environment did not select against the acquired trait.

These early biological studies influenced his view of mental evolution. "That experience taught me not to explain the whole of mental life by maturation alone!"[11] In other words, if a parallel exists between biological and cognitive functioning, then the interaction of organism and environment plays an explanatory role in both. The convergence of this biological thinking with the studies of childhood development provided the material from which his biological theory of knowledge and assessment of evolution derive. It is to this biological theory of knowledge that we now turn.

A Theory of Structures

In his autobiography Piaget mentioned two shortcomings of his early psychological research. First, his studies limited themselves to language. He had engaged children in conversation in order to understand their logic, despite his belief that logic proceeds from action. He had also assumed that language directly reflects actions and that understanding children's logic entails communicating with them verbally. Later he learned that this was not the case and that children's actions, at certain stages of development, display a logic that cannot be articulated. In other words, a child may be able to draw logical conclusions without being capable of verbalizing them. The other shortcoming was his inability to find structures corresponding to logical operations. Since this concept of structure was crucial for Piaget, and since its meaning developed throughout his work, we might pause to fix its meaning.

By considering intellectual evolution progressing through a series of qualitatively different stages, we might ask what characterizes a particular stage. Piaget argued that a stage is characterized by, among other things, a structure, literally the interrelatedness of parts within an organized totality or, in other words, an organization, form, or coordination. Thus structural properties form an integrated whole. He referred to the totality of a structure as a structure-of-the-whole (*structure d'ensemble*), itself characterized primarily by an equilibrium between the parts and the whole.

For instance, there are physical structures, such as the nervous system, eyes, and other organs, which effect the development of knowledge and which are transmitted by heredity. Automatic reflexes, the programmed responses to environmental stimuli like the sucking reflex, are also transmitted by heredity. It is only in newborn infants that actions depend on elementary behavioral structures. In addition to physical and elementary behavioral structures, there exist psychological structures. For example, a reflex to suck derives from hereditary structures, but thumb sucking derives from psychological structures, since the reflex to suck is not identical with bringing the hands toward the mouth. The latter is a regular, organized, coherent, and coordinated pattern of behavior; it is a learned behavior. But the child who performs a mathematical operation like addition also displays learned behavior. The ability to perform this operation exemplifies a complex structure. This activity reveals that older children have different structures, corresponding to the intellectual operations they are capable of performing. The child who can add, subtract, or classify objects clearly displays different psychological structures than infants. These structures are crucial to understanding Piaget's evolutionary theory, since intellectual development proceeds in terms of attaining the equilibrium that defines such structures.

Piaget usually uses the term structure to refer to any stable element in a biological system of development. When referring to cognitive development, he usually uses the term *schema* or its plural form *schemata* to denote the structured elements. A simple way of understanding a cognitive schema is to think of it as a concept or category. Much like a card in an index file, a schema helps process incoming information.

Alternatively, schema can be understood with reference to actions. Schemata are labeled according to the behavior to which they refer, hence we say "the schema of sucking" or "the schema of grasping." It is not quite correct to say that action and schemata are identical; rather actions apply schemata to reality. It is not merely that the infant grasps but that a cognitive structure exists which disposes the child to grasp repeatedly and thereby assimilate reality. But schemata are not identical with operations since operations are internalized generalizable actions. Operations imply the existence of the structures which make operations possible. Thus schemata are a necessary condition of actions and operations.

> The defining characteristic of a schema is its organization. The notion of structure, organization, and adaptation are intertwined as we will see in the next section. A schema initiates recognizable, recurrent, and organized behavior. The organized nature of schemata make possible the assimilation of different objects which serve as aliments to the schema. A living organism, its physical and psychological organs and their sub-components, mathematical groups, and scientific theories are all structures. They are all organized totalities and all characterized by three properties: wholeness, transformation laws, and self-regulation.[12]

A structure is a whole in the sense that it is more than the sum of its aggregate parts; in other words, it has properties that its parts do not possess. For instance, a mathematical structure has properties like associativity and commutativity, that individual integers do not. But the whole does not have properties prior to its parts, nor is it some mysterious thing unconnected to the parts. Rather, a whole is the sum of the parts and their relations, constituting what Piaget called composition laws. These laws give structure to the system and govern the kinds of transformations that can occur within it, for instance the laws governing mathematical, logical, or physical transformations. Finally, self-regulation characterizes structures. Self-regulation refers to a structure's ability to conserve its stability and maintain itself. This entails two characteristics: self-maintenance and closure. Self-maintenance refers to the fact that the structure's laws of transformation are preserved. Closure contributes to the structure's stability by guaranteeing that transformation will not be too great or rapid. Piaget said that these characteristics guarantee "that the transformations inherent in a structure never lead beyond the system but always engender elements that belong to it and preserve its laws."[13]

The idea of structure relates to other key concepts in Piaget's system. Structure can be opposed to function and content. The content refers to what the individual is thinking about or the manner in which one contemplates a given problem. This content manifests itself in observable behavior which reflects intellectual activity. Thus different persons answer questions differently based upon the content of their thought. The child, mechanic, or engineer give various answers to what makes a car go. If a child says it goes because it has horses inside, the contents of the child's thought differ from that of an adult, revealing different cognitive structures. Much of his early research was devoted to a determination of the content of children's thought.

The function of developing intelligence refers to the characteristics of intellectual activity which hold true everywhere and for everyone independent of their stage of development. While intellectual content and structure vary depending upon the level of development, intellectual functioning remains invariant. These invariant processes determine the course of evolution. It is to these functional invariants that we now turn.

The Functional Invariants

Convinced that cognition precedes language, Piaget observed children before they acquired language. He presented practical problems designed to elicit actions from children, which actually was closer to his own original postulate that logic originates out of action. The evidence derived from experiments confirmed the view that action paved the way for the developing intellect even before the appearance of language.

Observing the most primitive actions in newborn children brought Piaget close to the origins of intelligence and its dependency on biological functioning. He began his study by asserting that it would raise questions concerning the relationship between mind and biological organization. Since verbal abilities are based upon sensorimotor intelligence, relating to both sensory and motor aspects of bodily activity, and since sensorimotor intelligence in turn is based upon the organism's structure, there is a connection between mind and biological functioning. Mind presupposes the organism's morphogenesis—the evolution of its structural forms—because a continuity exists between mind and the organism's structure.

In what way are mind and morphogeny continuous? In the first place hereditary factors, like the nervous system and sensory organs, condition intellectual evolution. These might be regarded as structural aspects of intelligence. Our physical structures influence our most fundamental conceptions of the world; e.g., the wavelengths we see and the frequencies we hear. These structures derive from the fact that we are members of a species and inherit them. Piaget called these structural properties our specific heredity. While these properties make their contribution to our intellectual development, they cannot fully explain it. In fact, our knowledge goes well beyond the limitations imposed by our species-specific heredity. This first connection between biology and knowledge is important, but it cannot account for intellectual development.

Nonetheless there is something else we inherit besides our physical structure. By virtue of being a biological organism, we inherit certain functions which we share with other organisms and which constitute our general heredity. These inherited functions allow us to overcome the limitations imposed by our specific heredity and make intellectual progress. The mode of intellectual functioning that we inherit should not be confused with structures, since structures evolve through the course of development. Functions generate intellectual structures but the basic properties of intellectual functioning remain stable or unchanged. These properties are called *functional invariants*.

Piaget claimed that these functions impose necessary conditions on the developing structures. In other words, functions are prior to structures, since structures must be elaborated. The structures are the result of evolution and should not be thought of as "innate ideas." It is not the structures, but the inherited functions which make intellectual progress possible. The most important elements of our biological inheritance are the functions which allow structural limitations to be overcome. While Piaget devoted the majority of his early work to the details of structural changes between stages, he also considered the functioning which accounts for these changes. By considering functions, one uncovers the basic components of intellectual adaptation and, by extension, biological adaptation. "Intelligence is an adaptation."[14] So began Piaget's treatment of the functions common to both biological and cognitive functioning. Note that he is not saying merely that intelligence leads to adaptation, but that it *is* an adaptation.

> To say that intelligence is a particular instance of biological adaptation is thus to suppose that it is essentially an organization and that its function is to structure the universe just as the organism structures its immediate environment.[15]

In the same way the organism tries to adapt to the environment by constructing new physical forms, the intellect adapts by constructing new cognitive structures. What functions are common to both intellectual and biological behavior? Piaget named two invariants: *organization* and *adaptation*. All biological acts are adaptations to and organizations of the environment.

Let us begin with adaptation. While adaptation can be conceived as a state, Piaget thought of it as a process. In this process the organism is transformed in a way favorable to its preservation. Adaptation consists of two sub-components, *assimilation* and *accommodation*. Piaget conceptualized assimilation as follows. Let a, b, and c, be elements of some organized totality and let x, y, and z, be elements of the environment. He represented the process of assimilation as follows:

$$(1)\ a + x \rightarrow b;$$
$$(2)\ b + y \rightarrow c;$$
$$(3)\ c + z \rightarrow a,\ \text{etc.}$$

The process consists of incorporating the environmental elements into the existing structure and transforming those elements so that they comprise part of the structure. For example, food will be transformed to comprise part of the structure of the organism. The process is cyclic; the structure continues to assimilate new environmental elements to maintain its existence. Absorbing or accepting the environmental input into the existing structure was what he meant by assimilation. This process of assimilation applies to chemical reactions, physical transformations, sensorimotor behaviors, and cognitive functioning. This process does not destroy the input of the environment but transforms it.

Assimilation thus involves the organism dealing with the environment in terms of its existing structures. Biological or cognitive material is integrated and interpreted according to the existing schemata. Notice that the input is altered to fit the existing schemata in the process of assimilation and that assimilation accounts for the growth of schemata.

The second component of adaptation is accommodation. If the organism's structure is confronted with a different environmental input that it cannot assimilate, say x', then adaptation cannot occur. If the organism is able to assimilate x' then the organism will be modified. That is, the variation in input (x' instead of x) modifies the organism's structure so that it can adapt to the new stimulus. The process may be represented as follows:

$$(1)\ a + x' \rightarrow b';$$
$$(2)\ b' + y \rightarrow c;$$
$$(3)\ c + z \rightarrow a.$$

Accommodation means the modification of existing structures due to environmental changes. In this process, the modification of the organism compensates for the change in the environment. For adaptation to take place both assimilation, the organism's relatively passive reception of the environment, and accommodation, the organism's relatively active modification of its structures, must take place.

Accommodation fundamentally entails the transformation of structures in response to the environment. As we have stated, the organism attempts to assimilate new stimuli from the environment. If this is not possible, because no schemata exist to assimilate it, then a new schema must be created or an old one modified. In either case accommodation takes place. If neither of these can be achieved, extinction will occur. Accommodation results in a change of schemata, allowing for the new stimulus to be assimilated. Note how the existing schemata are altered by the input. It is this reciprocity or dynamic interactionism, input altered by existing schemata and existing schemata altered by input, which characterizes adaptation.

Piaget defined adaptation as "an equilibrium between assimilation and accommodation."[16] It is not difficult to see why this is the case. If the organism did nothing but assimilate, it would have a few very large schemata and not be able to differentiate between things. All assimilations would be forced into a few schemata. If the organism did nothing but accommodate, it would have a great number of small schemata but these would not be capable of generalization. All assimilations would be forced into different schemata. The balance between these processes is equilibrium.

Perhaps a simple biological example would provide clarification of the assimilation/accommodation process. The process of consuming nutrients from the environment is adaptive since the effect is to modify the organism in a way favorable to its preservation. This process can be distinguished conceptually in terms of two subprocesses. First, the environmental substances are incorporated into the structures of the organism, ie., assimilation. Second, the substances effect a subsequent transformation of the structures of the organism itself, i.e., accommodation. In the case of digestion, the organism incorporates and transforms the food with existing structures—assimilation—and the structures are modified by the demands of the food—accommodation. While the processes can be distinguished conceptually, in reality they are inseparable and together form the process of adaptation.

Cognitive adaptation is an extension of biological adaptation and can be understood in the same way. Individuals assimilate or incorporate external reality into their psychological structures and these structures subsequently modify or accommodate to the environmental demands. Cognitive adaptation is the accord or harmony of thought to things. Analogous to the organism's adaptation to the environment is the knower's adaptation to the known. The parallel with biology is striking, digestive and cognitive systems both assimilate and accommodate.

Both biological and cognitive functioning presuppose exchanges with the environment and an underlying organization within the subject. (While adaption is the external aspect of the process, organization is the internal aspect.) In general, organization refers to the tendency of species to organize their physical and/or psychological processes. For example, birds possess certain physical structures which allow them to function in the air. The interaction and coordination of these structures results from the bird's organizational tendencies. The tendency of infants to coordinate their looking and grasping schemata exemplify the organization of psychological structures. Organization then is the tendency, common to all forms of life, to coordinate and integrate internal structures.

Since intelligence is an extension of biological functioning, cognition also presupposes an underlying structure or organization. Whereas biological organization refers to morphology and is marked by different levels of biological development, intellectual organization refers to the interrelationships of intellectual operations and is marked by stages of cognitive development.

In summary, cognitive evolution occurs because of the invariant functions which are responsible for the direction of both biological and cognitive evolution. In simplest terms, the principles of cognitive evolution are the same as those of biological evolution.

Theories of Biological and Cognitive Evolution

Theories of Evolution

Both biological and cognitive development entail a relationship between organism and environment. As a result, theories that apply to one domain should be able to be extended to the other. In biology, these express themselves as theories of evolutionary adaptation; in cognition, as theories of intellectual development and epistemology. This follows if we remember that both intelligence and biological evolution are the adaptation of the organism to its surrounding environment. Biological theories of adaptation should illuminate theories of intellectual adaptation because the basic reflexes and morphology of the organs "constitute a sort of anticipatory knowledge of the external environment, an unconscious and entirely material knowledge but essential to the later development of real knowledge."[17] Piaget claimed that five theories are available to explain either biological and intellectual adaptation.[18] We will examine each in turn.

1) The first solution is *Lamarckism*. According to this theory adaptation occurs when the environment acts upon the organism, and the organism acquires characteristics in response without internal action. These acquired characteristics become hereditarily fixed and the accumulated changes result in evolution. The corresponding psychological/epistemological version is associationist-empiricism. In this theory knowledge results from associations of habits or ideas, and the object of knowledge is paramount, since knowledge consists in the imprint of the object on a passive subject. In other words, knowledge is not conditioned by the internal activity of the subject.

2) *Vitalism* is the view which attributes adaptation to a special internal power of the organism which construct organs. A preestablished harmony between the organism and environment exists, and an entelechy or vital force directs development. As a psychological theory intellectualism asserts that intelligence is an innate faculty, allowing for direct knowledge of objects not mediated by the subject.

The subject's powers are pre-structured or pre-given before any encounter with objects. This view corresponds to a naive realism in epistemology.

3) According to biological *preformism,* organic structures are innate, existing prior to contact with the environment. The corresponding psychological/epistemological theory is *apriorism,* the conviction that innate structures pre-exist in order to adapt the intellect to the world. Knowledge derives from the subject's preformed structures because these innate structures organize experience. The view is non-developmental since intelligence is regarded as a primary datum.

4) A fourth point of view is *mutationism* (Neo-Darwinism). This biological theory attributes evolutionary adaptation to the internal structure of the organism. Variations occur through random mutations which are then selected by the environment according to their survival value. The psychological counterpart is *pragmatism,* conventionalism or the theory of groping. Essentially, this is trial and error learning, where random ideas are tested for their pragmatic or convenience value. The trials or hypotheses begin with the subject and are then eliminated or preserved by experiences, ie., successes and failures. Primary emphasis is placed on the subject, who structures reality according to associations, habits, groupings, or conventions.

5) The final view, *biological relativity,* refers to the mutual interdependency between organism and environment. Adaptation occurs by the interaction between organism and environment. The organism neither passively reacts to the environment nor does it act upon the environment with preformed structures. Rather, the organism actively structures itself due to interaction with the environment which initiates a correlative morphogenesis. As a theory of intelligence, relativism supposes a union of subject and object. The subject's activity responds to the constitution of the object, as the object is constituted by the subject. Neither the subject nor the object is primary in the acquisition of knowledge. Because knowledge arises across time due to the interaction, this view is relativistic.

Based upon his study of *Limnaea,* Piaget believed that biological adaptation occurred according to this last model. The purpose of *The Origins of Intelligence in Children* (1936) was to determine which of these theories of adaptation accounted for intellectual development. The results of this inquiry provided Piaget the opportunity to advance his early assessment of the evolutionary process.

Observation and Theories Compared

Piaget's major discovery in *The Origins of Intelligence in Children* was that intelligence evolves through a series of stages.[19] The greater part of the work described his detailed observations of sensorimotor development in children. But by the end of these studies he was in a position to compare his observations with the theories of intelligence outlined above. We now turn to his conclusions.

Associationist-empiricism correctly emphasizes the role that experience plays in development. The theory is characterized by two basic beliefs: 1) it considers experience as imposing itself on a passive subject; and 2) it regards experience as independent of subjects. But empiricism—the view that reality impresses itself upon a receptive but passive subject—fails to explain the facts of development for three reasons. First, the facts suggest that the importance of experience increases with development. The infant's egocentrism prevents it from profiting by experience because its schemata are not sufficiently developed. As these schemata develop, the infant profits from the encounters with experience. But experience is not a homogeneous entity impressing itself upon a subject and, since the role played by experience changes with development, development appears to depend on more than experience. "Experience, accordingly, is not reception but progressive action and construction: This is the fundamental fact."[20]

The second reason is closely connected. If the subject cannot assimilate certain data, then the environment will not impress itself upon the subject, inasmuch as the activity of the subject determines what experiences will be (and can be) assimilated. Knowledge is not merely imposed upon the subject but actively constructed by the subject. Experience derives from and is non-existent without the subject's activity; it is not imposed exclusively from without. Our experiences progress to the extent that they are animated by the subject's cognitive activity. Thus, Piaget rejected all forms of empiricism or, as he sometimes calls them, *copy theories*.

> In other words, knowledge could not be a copy, since it is always a putting into relationship of object and subject, and incorporation of the object to the schemata which are due to activity itself and which simply accommodate themselves to it while making it comprehensible to the subject. To put it still differently, the object only exists, with regard to knowledge, in its relations with the subject and, if the mind always advanced more toward the conquest of things, this is because it organizes experience more and more actively, instead of mimicking, from without, a ready-made reality. The object is not a "known quantity" but the result of a construction.[21]

Finally, Piaget rejected all copy theories of knowledge because they claim that knowledge derives from elementary data and subsequent associations. But accommodation to an object presupposes assimilation to organized totalities. Observations convinced him that children's minds were organized totalities from the beginning and that the most primitive forms of contact with the external world stimulate development only if organized totalities exist to assimilate them. In essence, he rejected empiricism because the evidence indicates that an active subject constructs knowledge by assimilating it to schemata. Intellectual development is not a passive project, not possible without the active organization of the subject, and not a blank slate being filled.

The second theory that Piaget discussed was *vitalism-intellectualism*. As we have seen, intellectualism regards intelligence as a faculty or organizational form that is pre-given and which allows the subject to directly experience the object. The biological counterpart is vitalism, which postulates an entelechy which directs biological growth. Piaget uncovered some truth in the holistic and non-reductionistic elements of this approach but otherwise found the theory wanting.

In the first place, the whole of intelligence is irreducible and invariant according to this approach. Piaget's genetic approach rejected this idea, arguing that only functions are invariant. He had observed the remarkable transformations that occur during ontogenetic development and concluded that there is no inherent faculty transcending genetic causality. Second, intellectualism tends toward a realism. The function of the faculty of cognition directs itself toward an already-made reality which does not submit to the subject's transformations of it. But the facts contradict this, since at every stage development proceeds by a construction resulting from the interaction between the subject and objective reality.

He now turned to *apriorism-gestaltism*, which explains intelligence by the existence of categories or forms of thought which organize experience. He agreed with its emphasis on structured wholes, and he certainly agreed that the subject takes an active role in organizing reality.

The first major point of disagreement between Piaget and apriorism-gestaltism is in the concept of schema. "The schema is therefore a Gestalt which has a history."[22] Schemata are products of a long developmental history, and they have a continuity that Gestaltism does not allow. Even a dramatic "gestalt switch" would have a developmental history. Second, schemata extend themselves to fit new data. They are developmental whereas the range of Gestalten must be predetermined. Third, schemata result from the action of the subject, while Gestalt forms turn on and off as the field conditions change. Finally, schemata make their way slowly toward an adequate conception of reality, they are not necessarily more adequate than previous ones. Schemata are never absolute or aprioristic in the manner of Gestalt forms.

The essence of Piaget's case against a preformist biology or an aprioristic epistemology is that schemata are dynamic developmental totalities that result from the adaptation of the subject to a changing environment. Neither biological nor cognitive structures are fixed. Piaget's schemata organize the world similar to Kant's categories, but schemata—as opposed to Kantian categories—evolve. While the functional invariants do not change, they are still processes and their dynamism distinguishes them from a static notion of biological or cognitive categories.[23]

The final theory that Piaget addressed was the *theory of groping*; the theory that knowledge is produced essentially by accident, a succession of trials and errors and selection of such trials after the fact. Piaget agreed that the child "gropes" with reality, at least to the extent that assimilations and accommodations attempt to bring the child in contact with reality. But he distinguished two types of groping; systematic and non-systematic. Non-systematic groping is non-directed and the environment selects the behavior elicited according to its fortuitous effects. For example, a child encountering an object for the first time may accidentally manipulate it in the correct fashion. But systematic groping directs itself toward the goal of recognizing the probable outcomes of actions. While Piaget granted that the nature of groping is partly non-directed, he did not accept that groping is entirely non-directed. Even the child who correctly manipulates an object by chance relies on lower level schema, (pulling, pushing, grasping) that have developed in past adaptations to the environment. Groping cannot be completely non-directed because it is based upon sensorimotor schemata which themselves are based upon past accommodations. He rejected groping as he did all explanations of evolution based exclusively on chance. Meticulous observations of psychogenesis had convinced him that evolution did not proceed in this manner.

Piaget's own theory found truth in parts of all of these positions. He agreed with empiricism that experience modifies intellectual development, but he argued that cognition utilizes experience only to the extent that cognition is structured as a consequence of previous development. There are invariants in his theory, as there are in intellectualism, but invariants are processes not special faculties. Neither of these theories placed enough emphasis on the subject's activity in the course of evolution.

Like a gestaltist, he believed that totalities structure reality, but he argued that these totalities are dynamic, evolutionary, and developmental. He accepted, as did the theory of groping, the difficulty of coming to know reality and the role the subject plays in testing theories against reality. But such trials are never initiated in isolation from the environment; they are direct responses to organism-environment interaction. Both apriorism-gestaltism and empiricism emphasize the primacy of the subject in the course of evolution, while empiricist and vitalistic theories emphasize the object. An interactionist theory emphasizes the interaction of subject and object and renders the most adequate account of the development of cognitive structures in the individual.

The Early Assessment of Evolution

Interactionism

Piaget's own theory of intellectual adaptation is a form of interactionism—the view that existing schemata alter environmental input and environmental input alters existing schemata.[24] In other words, change in the environment affects the organism, just as change in the organism must effect a change in the environment. There is a mutual interdependency between the organism and the environment, and the interaction of these two brings about intellectual evolution.

These conclusions were the result of Piaget's exhaustive empirical studies. They had convinced him that the environment plays a role in determining the development of thought but that the child does not begin with a *tabula rasa*, since children bring a structure to any experience which influences the construction of reality. The four and ten year old, for example, have different structures which determine the nature of experience. But the role of the subject or knower is just as important as the role of the environment. Hence intellectual evolution results from the dynamic interaction of these two forces.

Perhaps an example might serve to illustrate how interactionism accounts for intellectual development. Examining the development of a complex idea like causality, we find various theories which attempt to explain the origin of the concept. For instance, Hume's theory of causality suggests that the idea of causality arose from the habitual association of events in the environment. Piaget agreed with Hume that the sights and sounds of objects play an instrumental role in the formation of the idea, but he disagreed that the environment "happens" to subjects, since the subject actively organizes experience when it is assimilated. Organizational activity, which is contingent upon the development of schemata, assures that the subject is not passive. Kant's notion that causality can be traced to a priori categories of the mind is no more adequate. There are no invariant structures; this is a fundamental thesis of a genetic understanding of causality and supported by decades of research. The only hypothesis consistent with the available evidence is that interactionism accounts for the idea of causality.

> Causality consists in an organization of the universe caused by the totality of relations established by action and then by representation between objects as well as between object and subject. Hence causality presupposes at all levels an interaction between the self and things . . . . [25]

From the beginning of life, the infant's basic functioning and primitive reflexes interact with the environment. The development of the infant's first acquired adaptations—sucking the thumb, following with the eyes, searching for sounds, and grasping objects—result from environmental stimuli and the subject's activity. Neither passive reception of stimuli nor any version of apriorism or preformism explains these adaptations.

Furthermore, intelligence does not appear out of nowhere; it is an extension of the organism's biological functioning. From this biological base, the processes of assimilation and accommodation move the subject toward a greater knowledge of both things and itself. Intellectual evolution progresses by acquiring external things and reflecting upon these acquisitions. Beginning in egocentrism, the initial biological state of the organism, the subject becomes gradually *decentered*. The epistemic subject comes to contemplate itself, regarding itself as an object. Subsequently, other epistemic objects emerge and eventually the whole world of mathematical, physical, and biological objects become known. Intelligence begins as an extension of biology, but in the end it will surpass biology by achieving knowledge of independent objects.

Intellectual evolution could result from the subject changing to adapt to the objects of knowledge, or from the objects of knowledge changing to adapt themselves to the structures of the subject. But both of these views are false. Theoretical speculations aside, observation shows that neither theory—empiricism or apriorism—accounts for the evidence. Knowledge evolves by the dynamic interaction of both the subject and the objects of its knowledge.

The Evolution of Cognition

The continual coordination of schemata characterizes cognitive evolution. As we have seen, schemata are malleable, that is, they continually change as assimilation and accommodation occur. While the details of this process need not concern us, the key idea is that interactionism explains both cognitive development and the growth of schemata.[26] While *The Origins of Intelligence in Children* had focused primarily on the role of assimilation in sensorimotor development, *The Construction of Reality in the Child* (1937) focused on accommodation and described how the categories of spatial relations, causality, object concept, and time proceed from sensorimotor activity.

Understanding the relationship between these processes completes our picture of Piaget's characterization of cognitive evolution in the first two years of life. Reflecting on the psychogenetic research that had spanned almost twenty years, by the late 1930s, Piaget affirmed:

> These global transformations of the objects of perception, and of the very intelligence which makes them, gradually denote the existence of a sort of law of evolution, which can be phrased as follows: assimilation and accommodation proceed from a state of chaotic undifferentiation to a state of differentiation with correlative coordination.[27]

Here we recognize the centrality Piaget conferred on the idea that evolution is a gradual organization from chaos to order. In general, cognitive evolution moves from a state of egocentrism, where assimilation and accommodation are undifferentiated and antagonistic, to a state of objectivity and equilibrium, where the two are distinct and coordinated. In the sucking schema, for instance, assimilation and accommodation of an object remain undifferentiated. It is only much later that the action and the object of the action are differentiated. There is also an antagonism between functions; assimilation directed toward the familiar, accommodation toward the novel.

The process of cognitive evolution is exceedingly difficult because early on the child's cognitive schemata are inadequate for adaptation. Children must continually accommodate in order to assimilate new objects especially if they cannot differentiate between these processes. Needless to say, this is frustrating! But from this primitive egocentrism—where assimilation of objects to self is not distinguishable from accommodation of self to objects—develops individuals who delight in accommodation. As these accommodations multiply and transform schemata, the subject becomes interested in novelty. The process is reciprocal. On the one hand, assimilation of novel reality to the subject's schemata brings about accommodation and, on the other hand, accommodation to reality brings about novel assimilatory structures. An equilibrium between assimilation and accommodation results, and the growth and development of schemata ensue. Functional processes stimulate cognitive evolution.

> In the last analysis, it is this process of forming relationships between a universe constantly becoming more external to the self and an intellectual activity progressing internally which explains the evolution of the real categories.[28]

In addition, the subject places itself among the multiplicity of objects as cognitive evolution proceeds. As a consequence, a harmony between subjective organization and objective experience results, and "the subject's perspective of the universe is radically transformed; from the integral egocentrism to objectivity is the law of that evolution."[29]

We are now in position to summarize Piaget's early assessment of cognitive evolution. His first studies revealed that cognitive structures evolve due to the interaction of the organism and environment, a conclusion consistent with his early biological research with mollusks. But why do cognitive and biological structures evolve analogously? Because knowledge extends biological functioning and both processes are governed by invariant functions. These functions precipitate the organism/environment interaction that results—specifically in cognitive evolution—in a continual decentering. He concluded that the functional invariants account for the process and direction of cognitive evolution.

The Early Assessment of Evolution

These conclusions concerning cognitive evolution derived from Piaget's studies in psychogenesis and were consistent with his biological research. This consistency convinced him that neither Lamarckism nor Darwinism were adequate evolutionary models. Despite revising many of his theories, the theory of equilibration as a case in point, he never wavered throughout his career in the belief that neither Lamarckism nor Darwinism were completely correct.

To complete our picture of Piaget's early account of evolution, we need a more detailed analysis of the biological evidence that informed his view. How can one explain the behavior of the aquatic mollusk, the *Limnaea stagnalis*? We might suppose that the mollusks' shortened and globular shape is a phenotypic adaptation to the turbulent waters. However, since this shape becomes hereditarily fixed—it does not revert to the elongated shape when bred in still waters—it is not merely an adaptation of the phenotype.

It might appear that Lamarckism provides the solution to the problem. The mollusks acquired hereditary traits which were stimulated by environmental action, and the phenotypic adaptation, a shortened and globular shape, became a part of the genotype when this trait was transmitted by heredity. If this took place, *Limnaea stagnalis* would provide an example of Lamarck's inheritance of acquired characteristics. However, Piaget found this solution untenable. When bred under experimental conditions, contractions of the shape occurred, but they were not transmitted to the genotype. The influence of environmental factors upon heredity depends, he thought, on the intensity and duration of the environmental stimuli, correlative with an activity of the organism in response to the environmental stress.

Non-evolutionary views cannot account for such adaptation either. If vitalism or preformism were the case, the organism would immediately solve its problems and it would not take many centuries for the phenotypic adaptation to appear. It must then be that mutationism, the Darwinian solution, resolves the problem. According to this solution, genotypic changes bring about phenotypic ones. Random changes in the genotype produce some individuals with traits—in this case globular shapes—that increase their chances for survival in turbulent waters. These chance mutations happen independent of the environment and so there is no environmental action on genotypes.

But significant problems present themselves for this solution. In the first place, mollusks with globular shapes can exist in various lacustrine environments, but in fact they exist only where they are best adapted. If chance mutations explain adaptation then we should find the globular variety randomly distributed. The fact that they exist only where environmental conditions are favorable is evidence of the organism's active response to the environment. In the second place, the environment does not select against the acquired trait, since the globular shape does not disappear when the mollusks are reintroduced into still waters, even when observed over long periods of time.

By the late 1930s, Piaget had concluded that the Lamarckian solution in biology and the empiricist solution in epistemology were untenable. Neither biological nor cognitive evolution result solely from exogenous factors exerted upon the organism. On the other hand, he concluded that neither Darwinism nor any variety of apriorism or pragmatism could explain the facts.[30] Evolution does not result solely from the endogenous activity of the organism. Evolution, both biological and cognitive, results from a continual and dynamic interaction between the organism and environment.

Piaget's early assessment of evolution resulted from the research on psychogenesis and biology conducted and published for the most part during the 1920s and 1930s. During the 1940s, numerous volumes were published dealing with the development in children of the concepts of time, velocity, chance, spatial relations, and geometric concepts, just to name a few.[31] This research confirmed his earlier findings that cognitive concepts and the adaptation they represent result from an interactionism. They also confirmed some of his earliest ideas concerning structures, specifically, that they are actions internalized as operations and forms of equilibrium. Piaget described the stages of structural evolution leading to adult cognition in the same way as the embryologist might describe morphogenesis:

> Our task is therefore clear: we must now reconstruct the develop-
> ment of intelligence, or the stages in its formation, until we are able
> to account for the final operational level whose forms of equilib-
> rium we have just been describing.... Briefly then, the explanation
> of intelligence amounts to linking the higher operations with the
> whole process of development, development being regarded as an
> evolution governed by an inherent need for equilibrium.[32]

From this point on, the concept of equilibrium played an increasingly important role in his conception of evolution. In the early 1950s, Piaget reflected upon thirty years of research.

> My one idea, developed under various aspects in (alas!) twenty-two
> volumes, has been that intellectual operations proceed in terms of
> structures-of-the-whole. These structures denote the kinds of equi-
> librium toward which evolution in its entirety is striving; at once
> organic, psychological and social, their roots reach down as far as
> biological morphogenesis itself.[34]

Piaget's next task was to determine if his conception of evolution was applicable to the history and epistemology of the sciences. It is to these investigations that we now turn.

CHAPTER 3

The Circle of the Sciences: Introduction to Genetic Epistemology

By the early 1950s Piaget was ready to interpret his research on the development of scientific concepts in children in the light of classical epistemologies. While his empirical investigations in the intervening decades had focused primarily on the ontogenesis of knowledge, he now turned his attention to the phylogenesis of knowledge. In the same way that psychogenesis revealed how these concepts develop in children, the historico-critical method would reveal how scientific concepts develop in history. In both cases, he would apply the evidence—either psychogenetic or historical—to epistemological problems.

We have already seen how psychogenesis elucidates epistemological issues. Similarly, the historico-critical method illuminates concepts in the history of science, (number, space, speed, time, motion, force, etc.) from a developmental or historical perspective. In both domains, the evidence reveals that concepts have a developmental history. Besides, the biological model of intelligence predicts a parallelism between ontogenesis and phylogenesis. This same model also implies that knowledge is a biological adaptation rooted in sensorimotor behaviors and that theories of the evolution of knowledge parallel theories of the evolution of life—since knowledge is an extension of life itself. Thus we should not be surprised to uncover a parallelism between the ontogenesis and the phylogenesis of knowledge.

Genetic Epistemology

Piaget called the discipline that studies the development of knowledge in both the individual and the group *genetic epistemology*. While an epistemologist is interested in the complex relationship between the knower and the known, a genetic epistemologist investigates the developmental and historical aspects of this relationship. Piaget always claimed that he was not a psychologist, but a genetic epistemologist.[1]

In the first volume of *Introduction à l'épistémologie génétique* (1950), Piaget proclaimed that "the genetic method undertakes the study of knowledge with regard to its real construction."[2] And he defined genetic epistemology as "the study of the passage from states of lesser knowledge to states of more advanced or superior knowledge."[3] But if knowledge progresses, what mechanisms are responsible for this growth? The quest for these mechanisms led him to another definition of genetic epistemology.

> From this point of view, one could define genetic epistemology in a broader and more general way as the study of the mechanisms whereby bodies of knowledge grow. The essential function of this discipline would then be to analyze, in all areas involving the genesis or elaboration of scientific bodies of knowledge, the passage from states of lesser knowledge to states of more advanced knowledge. In a word, genetic epistemology would constitute an application, to the study of bodies of knowledge, of the experimental method . . .[4]

In short, genetic epistemology is that discipline which applies a developmental or historical perspective to bodies of knowledge. We can further clarify the discipline by considering its scope.[5] In the broadest sense genetic epistemology encompasses: 1) the ontogenesis of knowledge—the development of knowledge in the individual; and 2) the phylogenesis of knowledge—the development of knowledge in history, particularly in the sciences. The phylogenesis of knowledge may be subdivided into: 2a) the historical or developmental aspects of science; and 2b) the epistemological status of scientific knowledge. We will consider each in turn.

The historical method involves the use of developmental concepts (equilibration, egocentrism, decentration, reversibility, etc.) to explain the history of the sciences across time, i.e., a diachronic analysis. The epistemology of scientific knowledge concerns scientific knowledge at a given time, i.e., a synchronic analysis. This latter field permits of a twofold division depending upon whether we consider: 2bi) the epistemological status of a given science; or 2bii) the epistemological status of the relationships between the sciences. Again, we will consider each in turn.

The first area (2bi) asks the following epistemological questions about a given science, say mathematics. How does the necessity of mathematics derive from a contingent intellect? Why does mathematics apply to reality? And what is the epistemological status of mathematical concepts? The second area (2bii) considers the relationship between the sciences and asks: What is the origin and status of knowledge in different scientific fields? What is the relationship between the role played by the subject and the role played by the object in the constitution of knowledge in the various sciences? What is the nature of the relationship of the sciences to each other? We summarize the scope of genetic epistemology thus:

1. Growth of individual knowledge (ontogenesis)
2. Growth of collective knowledge (phylogenesis)
   a. History of the sciences
   b. Epistemology of the sciences
      i. Epistemology of a particular science
      ii. Epistemology of the relationships between sciences
3. Growth of other knowledge

The most explicit and complete discussion of the aims and methods of Piaget's genetic epistemology can be found in the introduction to his as-yet-untranslated magnum opus, *Introduction à l'épistémologie génétique*. There he argued that epistemology needs to be scientific. That is, we must utilize psychogenesis—the development of cognitive structures in the individual—as the key to understanding historiogenesis—the historical genesis of scientific knowledge.

Not surprisingly, Piaget turned to biology to specify the connection between psychogenesis and historiogenesis. Biologists study comparative anatomy in mature organisms by comparing species and their phylogeny. The analogous study in embryology compares individuals and their ontogeny. In the same way, genetic epistemologists study cognitive development by observing individuals and their psychogenesis, and they study comparative mental anatomy in science by analyzing scientific concepts and their historiogenesis. While the study of psychogenesis constitutes an ontogeny of reason, the study of historiogenesis constitutes a phylogeny of reason. This analogy is crucial for Piaget's entire project, since many of the conclusions drawn regarding the growth of scientific knowledge are based upon the evidence derived from the study of psychogenesis.

Piaget believed that in both psychogenesis and the history of science the subject tends toward a state of cognitive equilibrium. This tendency to push toward equilibrium continually adapts the organism to its cognitive environment. But what precisely is the relationship between equilibrium and the growth of knowledge?

Equilibration and Limit

Essentially, genetic epistemology investigates the process by which higher states of cognitive equilibrium are achieved. It portrays the process of cognitive evolution and uncovers the laws or mechanisms which govern it. But how can various sciences be said to achieve equilibrium? And is the equilibrium achieved by scientific knowledge partial and temporal or complete and atemporal? To answer these questions—and to further explicate the exact relationship between equilibrium and the growth of knowledge—Piaget introduced a concept to which he often returned. The concept of a *limit*.

> Supposing, as we have just admitted, that all genetic series lead toward certain equilibrium states, operating at the junction between the temporal real and non-temporal logic, a new problem arises for genetic methodology: can one consider all knowledge growth, in the history of the sciences or in psychological development, as leading toward a "limit"? And, to admit that is the case as far as certain particular and circumscribed series are concerned, it is possible to conceive, starting from the confrontation of a sufficient number of such series, the verification of a general epistemological hypothesis concerning knowledge as a whole . . . .
>
> The problem is thus the following: how to integrate in one or several large series, the study of individual knowledge growth, at first analyzed separately, and especially how to conceive a study of the convergence of these series so as to be able to speak of passage to a limit?[6]

Here Piaget confronted the problem of reconciling logic and time. Equilibrium is reached in a temporal process, but logic transcends time because of its stability and permanence. Equilibrium has the characteristics of both; it is stable and yet temporary. Can this tension be resolved by considering the growth of knowledge as a limit to be approached but never attained? Would the idea of a limit reconcile the increasing stability of knowledge with the temporal process? Whether we consider the ontogenesis of knowledge or the evolution of knowledge in any separate scientific field, we observe that knowledge develops toward a limit, that is, the limit of our current knowledge.

> The analysis of a notion's development allows in general the determination of successive levels of construction and the succession of these levels themselves constitutes a first type of series from which one can determine the law of formation. In this case [the development of the individual's knowledge] one can speak without metaphor of a genetic series and its convergence towards a certain limit, defined by a form of equilibrium . . . .[7]

But does knowledge as a whole develop toward a limit? And is this idea nothing but philosophical speculation? Piaget agreed that extending the results of his psychogenetic investigation to knowledge as a whole is problematic.

> Without any doubt evolution thus reached by genetic analysis, on the inside of the sector, reveals a transformation of the subject's intellectual capacities, and in correlation with this construction of new capacities, a transformation of the experience itself, that is to say of the reality such as it appears to the subject. But it goes without saying that these transformations of thought and the apparently real taken individually and collectively (that is to say relative to a determined level of this thought), as interesting as they are revealed to be with regard to the growth mechanism of knowledge, would not be able to bring about a generalizing formula, the reason being that the formula charged with expressing them will itself be relative to the reference system adopted by the observer, that is to say by the psychologist or the historian who studies these transformations from the outside relying upon his own knowledge.[8]

Genetic epistemologists study the stages of development and establish the transformation laws and eventual limit of the series. But their system of reference when studying the growth of scientific knowledge is contemporary science, and this system of reference is itself evolving. Hence it is difficult to establish a general law of the evolution of knowledge since the observer, in this case the genetic epistemologist, has no privileged perspective from which to judge the evolution of all of the sciences. Moreover, the genetic epistemologist utilizes psychology, mathematics, biology, etc. But these sciences are themselves just evolving systems of reference without any absolute foundation. Therefore, how do we know that they are advancing toward a limit? And how does the genetic epistemologist surpass the limits imposed by an evolving reference system and establish the laws governing the evolution of all knowledge? Piaget formulated this problem as follows:

If genetic analysis necessarily relies on a reference system formed by the sciences established at the moment considered, there would naturally arise a question of explaining this reference system in its turn, in order to generalize the genetic explication for all knowledge. But the following alternatives can then be presented: either genetic analysis will not succeed in realizing its own reference system and will therefore fail in constituting a general epistemology, or else it will succeed in doing so, but at the price of an evident circle, genetic analysis relying on, in this second case, a reference system which will be dependent itself on the same analysis.[9]

Piaget adopted the second alternative to resolve the problem of reference points. One science at one particular time does not take precedence over the others nor are the others all reducible to one particular science. Individually, no one science functions as the reference point. Rather the sciences are interdependent, and different forms of scientific explanation comprise a closed circle.

One can therefore extend without end the chain without exiting the circle, but the more the latter is enlarged the more the observed convergencies allow us to find in this growing coherence the assurance that the circle is not vicious.[10]

How might one construe this circular relationship among the scientific disciplines? To answer this question, Piaget advanced a notion to which he returned continually throughout his writings; the idea of *the circle of the sciences*.

It is true that the relations between the sciences are customarily understood as being characterized by a rectilinear series: mathematics, physics, (in the broad sense), biology and the psychosociological sciences would thus succeed each other according to a hierarchic principle such as the famous series of increasing complexity and decreasing generality conceived by August Comte. But then two questions arise. In the first place, what is mathematics founded on? On nothing other than itself, it is said, or on logic, which also relies on nothing other than itself. But if that can appear clear from one point of view, be it metaphysical, or strictly axiomatic, this ceases to be satisfactory as soon as one examines the conditions that render an axiomatic system possible. One therefore necessarily arrives at resorting to the laws of the human mind, which is an explicit (H. Poincaré, L. Brunschvicg, etc.) or implicit appeal to psychology. In the second place, and at the other extreme of the series, where does research in genetic psychology end? Precisely at explaining to us how intuitions and notions of space, number, order, etc., are constructed, that is to say in logical operations and mathematics. As soon as one no longer has a normative or a pure axiomatic point of view, the linear series of knowledge therefore becomes in reality circular because the series line, initially straight, slowly closes on itself.[11]

If we believe that knowledge rests on axiomatic principles of logic, as Aristotle did, we forget that the conditions which allow for such axioms are psychological. And psychology investigates mathematical and logical concepts.

The explications of psychology sooner or later refer themselves to those of biology; the latter rest in turn on those of psychochemistry; the physical explications rely themselves on mathematics; as for mathematics and logic, they could only be founded on the laws of the mind which are the object of psychology.[12]

To say that mathematics rests upon psychology means that an epistemology of mathematics relies upon psychological structures. Mathematics and logic are human constructions. Of course we can consider logical operations axiomatic first principles. But this makes psychological constructions axiomatic since the rules of logic and mathematics rely on the intellectual structures that construct them. In addition, these psychological structures are related in the opposite direction to biology, chemistry, and physics—to the circle of the sciences. The circle implies, most importantly, that the sciences grow together and that no scientific description of reality is more fundamental than any other. Piaget took great care in setting forth this fundamental idea.

This hypothesis [that the sciences form a circle] comes back to the supposition that scientific thought is constantly engaged in two simultaneous and complementary directions, which hold together the circle of the subject and the object. By mathematics and psychology, science assimilates reality to the framework of the human mind and thus follows an idealistic direction. In fact, on the one hand, mathematics assimilates sensible data to spatial and numerical schemata and therefore submits matter to a system of operations that is always more complex and more coherent, which allows deduction to dominate experience and even to explain it. On the other hand, psychology analyzes the operations and deliberately focuses on the subject's activity, which remains irreducible to a simple submission to the data of outside reality. But if this is one of the two constant directions of scientific thought, the other is no less clear. In physics and biology, science obeys a realistic tendency, which in turn subordinates the mind to reality. Biology therefore shows the connections of perception, motive power, and intelligence itself with the structure of the organism, while physics-chemistry put the organism into a world of material realities that are always more distanced from the immediate conscious states and in this aspect knowledge is centered on the object.

Whether one considers the circle of the sciences in one direction or the other, the object is accordingly reduced to the subject or the subject to the object. Science is therefore neither purely realistic nor purely idealistic, but oriented in the two directions at the same time, without it being legitimately possible to anticipate the final state of such a process.[13]

Mathematics and psychology are idealistic because they assimilate reality to existing schemata. Biology and physics are realistic because they accommodate the subject to the objects of knowledge. Knowledge results from the interaction of subject and object which stimulates the processes of assimilation and accommodation. The same processes that are at work in the sciences are also at work in the relationship between individual subject and object. The subject comes to know the object by assimilating it to schemata and by accommodating schemata to the objects of knowledge. Knowledge, either individual or scientific, never results exclusively from an *a priori* assimilatory idealism or an empirical accommodative realism. It results from the unceasing interplay between assimilation and accommodation, between subjects and objects.

Since the final state of knowledge would have to be known in order for epistemology to be complete, epistemology must remain "open" to future possibilities. What then guarantees the progress of knowledge? Precisely the fact that the circle is not vicious and that the growth of one kind of knowledge effects the others. The circular relationship between the sciences makes possible their collective growth.

> In making explicit the cyclic character of these relations [between the sciences], genetic epistemology therefore contributes, in the end, to making evident the profound reasons for the circle of the subject and object, a circle that is indefinitely extended by scientific research itself and which, once closed by the limit,—but a limit perhaps impossible to reach—will deliver the secret of human knowledge.[14]

Restricted and Generalized Genetic Epistemology

Piaget concluded his introduction to genetic epistemology by distinguishing between *restricted* and *generalized* genetic epistemology. This distinction further clarifies the issue of the system of reference or the norm by which the development of knowledge is measured. In restricted genetic epistemology, the reference point which measures the development of knowledge is the current state of knowledge in that science. For example, adult knowledge serves as a reference point to measure the development a child's knowledge, and, similarly, the current state of scientific knowledge serves as the reference point for historical scientific theories. But questions concerning whether these reference points are absolute and immutable are irrelevant. The system of reference is assumed to be fixed, stable, external, and objective. In a restricted genetic epistemology, development is not particularly problematic.

Generalized genetic epistemology does not assume such a norm. It recognizes that the reference point, now the circle of the sciences, is itself in motion as scientific conceptions of reality change. One can no longer distinguish between the object of genetic investigation—the growth of knowledge—and the frame of reference—the circle of the sciences—since both are in motion. For this reason we must remain open to the possibility that scientific thinking will eventually reveal a reality enormously different than the one we now envision. Generalized genetic epistemology investigates the evolution of this metaphysical system of reference. In Piaget's own words, it is "precisely the directions or 'vectors' inherent in the very progress of the sciences . . . that supply the research field to generalized genetic epistemology."[15] He proceeded to resolve the problem of reference points for a generalized genetic epistemology.

> Even though our present actual frame of mind, constituted by what we consider today to be true, is provisional and relative, it is always the case that, although we lack foreknowledge or exact assurance of the future, we can compare the present level to previous ones and make explicit the orientation which characterizes the pattern of known development. This determination of the general laws of evolution constitutes only a generalization of the method proper to restricted genetic epistemology, but this generalization supplies something to lean on, which seemed to be lacking with the abandoning of the reference system that the restricted system was using. It is therefore such a generalization, or search for the set of construction laws, which allows us to make the passage to the boundary which genetic epistemology makes its final goal, and this without being unfaithful to the psychogenetic and historico-critical methods, since this last problem prolongs if anything the "restricted" questions.[16]

The key to solving the problem is to generalize the results of restricted genetic epistemology so that they may be applicable to resolving issues concerning the evolution of all knowledge. At the same time, the generalization of the results of restricted genetic epistemology justifies the use of the psychogenetic and historico-critical methods, since it is in restricted genetic epistemology that development is most readily apparent. Still, one might too easily extend the laws discovered by restricted epistemology to generalized epistemology. In order to avoid this, and to maintain the objectivity of the genetic analysis given the relativity of systems of reference, Piaget issued two precautions. First, one cannot suppose, *a priori*, that there is any directionality or teleology in the development of science. Second, one cannot predict the future course of science; one can only describe the history of its development.

> The eventual discovery of a law of evolution in the field of scientific thought can naturally have value only up to the period in which that law was found. Retrospective interpolation is dangerous, but extrapolation regarding the future is quite illegitimate . . . . [17]

If the evolution of knowledge is *orthogenetic*—that is, progressive in a certain direction—this directionality can only be discovered after the fact by examining its history. Compared with restricted genetic epistemology, generalized genetic epistemology defers from making claims about the progress or direction of evolution since there is no standard against which such progress can be measured. The genetic epistemologist may uncover a directionality in individual's psychogenesis or the history of science a posteriori, but one cannot presuppose, a priori, that such directionality exists. Both precautions reiterate Piaget's commitment to an a posteriori analysis. "Our two rules are to reject both anticipation and the a priori method."[18]

Generalized genetic epistemology must determine if there are general evolutionary laws governing the growth of scientific knowledge. Piaget had already determined that evolutionary laws govern the ontogenesis of knowledge, particularly of scientific concepts. Now he had to determine if the development of scientific concepts in the history of science revealed a similar process. To do this he engaged in a historical analysis of the development of concepts in various sciences.

The Epistemology of the Sciences

The Epistemology of Mathematics

Piaget began his discussion in the first volume of *Introduction à l'épistémologie génétique* by considering the main questions of interest to a genetic epistemology of mathematics. First, how does one explain the genesis of mathematics? And second, how does one explain the correspondence of mathematics with reality? He was interested in both the genesis of mathematics and its epistemic power; the investigation of which he believed would reveal mathematics a paradigm of the evolution of knowledge.

Having introduced the basic aims of a genetic epistemology of mathematics, Piaget turned to recapitulating his research on the development of the concept of number in children. Empiricist theories fail to account for the genesis of number because number cannot be abstracted from objects. Innatist theories fail to account for this genesis because the concept of number develops. In dialectical fashion, he compared his own theory of number with competing theories. The mathematical logicism of Russell and Whitehead was deficient because they define number in terms of quantitative classes, in effect, begging the question of the definition of number and its genesis. In addition, he invoked Gödel's critique of mathematical foundationalism to support his position against the logicists.[19] He also criticized Poincaré's mathematical intuitionism because the evidence shows that the concept of number develops only after the necessary structures are in place; there is no intuition of number without previous coordinations of actions.

Against both theories, Piaget advanced his own operatory theory of number. The concept of number results from subjects reflecting on operations that they perform on objects. Primarily, this consists in the recognition of identity ($1 = 1$), the skill of classification ($1 < 1 + 1$), and the ability to place objects in a series ($1, 2, 3$, etc.). The key is that the concept of number evolves by reflection on operations; it is neither pregiven in reflections upon intuitions nor abstracted from reflections upon objects.

In order to distinguish the type of reflection operative in the evolution of mathematics, Piaget distinguished between *empirical abstraction* and *reflective abstraction*. Empirical abstraction occurs when the subject abstracts a property, characteristic, or aspect of some physical object or external reality and imagines this aspect to exist outside that object. For example, the shape, color, or texture can be abstracted from a physical object by coming in contact with it. Empirical abstraction consists in nothing more than deriving common characteristics, like redness or roundness, from a class of objects.

Reflective abstraction involves reflection about unobservable relationships, primarily logical and mathematical ones, constructed by the mind. Such abstractions do not depend upon observations but upon properties of operations—mathematical and logical laws— since the properties abstracted are not properties of objects. For instance, logical necessity does not arise from observation but from reflecting on actions or operations. Reflective abstraction involves a projection onto a higher level than has been previously attained; *it is a new construction*. The concept of number and the stages of cognitive development proceed according to reflective abstractions. Reflections on sensorimotor activity lead to cognitive representations, concrete operations derive from reflections on cognitive representations, and formal operations from reflections on concrete operations. During this process lower level knowledge is not destroyed but integrated into the higher level which surpasses it. Cognitive evolution consists in the construction of new knowledge based upon previous constructions by a process of reflective abstraction. Reflective abstraction is the driving force behind equilibration. It explains the growth of knowledge and is crucial to understanding how evolution reaches progressively higher and more complex levels of development.

Piaget also believed that this process explains the development of mathematics. Natural numbers and integers develop by the process of reflective abstraction, as do fractions, negative numbers, and imaginary numbers. Obviously negative and imaginary numbers do not depend upon objects but on reflections on operations. Negative numbers result by generalizing an operation—like addition or subtraction—in both directions on the number line. By positing negative numbers, a limitation to this generalization is removed. To take another example, the operation of deriving the square root is limited because it does not appear applicable to negative numbers and certain integers. We may overcome this limitation by postulating the imaginary and irrational numbers. Generalizing operations in this way is the essence of reflective abstraction. Generalizing the operation of subtraction, we construct negative numbers; generalizing the operation of square roots, we construct irrational and imaginary numbers. These generalizations do more than classify objects on the basis of their properties; they construct something new. Having discovered that the concept of number evolves by generalizing operations, Piaget turned to the historiogenesis of mathematics to determine if a similar evolution could be detected. Does the history of mathematics display an increasing awareness of the role that operations play in mathematical constructions?

Piaget's survey of the history of mathematics was designed to find out if its history does in fact parallel the development of mathematical concepts in the individual. In large part this is precisely what he did find. Consider that Egyptian mathematics was empirical or utilitarian, since it was used primarily to count and classify objects. Greek mathematics was based on deductive reasoning, but the Greeks— particularly Plato and Pythagoras—located mathematical objects outside the subject. As a consequence the development of their mathematics was limited because they did not recognize that formal thinking was operational, i.e., the result of interiorized action. This mathematical realism was gradually overcome by subsequent operatory generalizations. Algebra generalized mathematical operations from numbers to variables, thus freeing the form (variables) from the content (numbers) by a process of reflective abstraction. Analytic geometry extended the generalization to geometry; the theory of functions reflected the recognition of the operations themselves; and the theory of groups implied the structure-of-the-whole uniting all of these operations to each other. The history of mathematics reveals a growing awareness (*prise de conscience*) of the ability of mathematical operations to be generalized. Most importantly for Piaget, the historical development of mathematical concepts parallels their development in individuals. Greek mathematics corresponds to preoperational thinking, algebra and analytic geometry to concrete operations, and nineteenth-century mathematics to formal operations. This parallelism provided evidence that the model of evolution that applied to the individual knower could be extended to the history of science.

But if actions and reflections about them are at the basis of mathematics, then mathematics results from subjective constructions. Why then is mathematics not pure fantasy? Piaget rejected the view that mathematics corresponds to reality because it is based on external objects—empiricism—or because it derives exclusively from innate structures—apriorism. Rather, it is that mathematics has its origins in operations rooted in action which accounts for the relationship between mathematics and reality. These actions, and the operations that derive from them, are accommodated to reality. Thus a continuity exists stretching from formal operations, to more primitive operations, to general coordinations of actions, to the organism's basic biological structure, and finally to the universe being assimilated. This continuity accounts for the link between mathematics and reality. Mathematical thinking originates in the invariant functions while, at the same time, surpassing them by reflective abstractions.

One might argue that the continuity between the subject's formal operations and its organic structure is too weak to sustain the argument that mathematics corresponds to reality.[20] Whatever the relationship of organic structures to physical reality, why suppose that formal operations, which are so far removed from organic structures, relate to reality? Piaget answered that reflective abstractions never invalidate structures constructed at previous levels but incorporate them into a higher synthesis. This preserves the continuity between the organism's operations, its initial organic structures, and reality. Furthermore, inasmuch as the organism is an organized system which exists in dynamic interaction with the environment and that organization refers to the internal process of continual adaptation, it follows that knowledge of the external world is mediated by logico-mathematical structures. The organism's dynamic interaction with the environment guarantees that its organization ultimately reflects the physical reality with which it interacts.

The developmental and historical aspects of mathematical thinking demonstrate that a fundamental and similar process of evolutionary change is at work in both domains. The history of science provides evidence to conclude that the evolutionary model can be extended from psychogenesis to historiogenesis. This process of evolutionary change involves generalizing operations by a process of reflective abstraction, and this accounts for both the novelty and continuity of mathematical thinking. In addition, the constructions of mathematical thinking correspond to reality, thereby showing that the process is progressive.

The Epistemology of Physics

In the second volume of *Introduction à l'épistémologie génétique*, Piaget turned to the physical sciences. While mathematical knowledge originates by abstracting from actions, physical knowledge develops by abstracting from the accommodations of action to objects. Physics, as the most developed of the physical sciences, has characteristics of both mathematical and physical knowledge. Unlike mathematics, physics accommodates to the properties of objects but, like mathematics, it assimilates reality to operatory schemata. Physics has a dual character. When it is mathematical and idealistic, it emphasizes the assimilation of reality to the operatory schema of the subject. When it is empirical and realistic, it emphasizes the accommodation of the subject to physical objects.

To illustrate the dual nature of physics, Piaget considered the development of the notions of time, speed, and force. We might suppose that physical knowledge originates in sense experience—accommodation of schemata to objects, i.e., empiricism—or from internal intuitions of physical properties—assimilation of objects to schemata, i.e., apriorism. But he argued that psychogenetic research does not support either position. Experimentation reveals that physical knowledge derives from the union of logico-mathematical structures and the facts of experience. For example, the concept of time does not derive exclusively from experience or from primitive intuitions. Physical time results from the assimilation of events to operatory schemata, and psychological time results from a reflection upon these operations. Children do not have an intuition of time, nor is it derived without the prior development of schemata. The development of time provides an example of how the interaction between experience and schemata leads to the development of physical knowledge.

The theory of time is of particular interest because it has undergone a remarkable transformation in the twentieth century in relativity theory. Piaget claimed that a genetic analysis of time illuminates these developments. His experiments established that the idea of simultaneity is decisive in the development of the concept of time, but physical law prevents simultaneity from applying on the cosmic scale. This fact exposes how the concept of time is operationally constructed and, at the simultaneously, constrained by reality. This development also reveals the extent to which both the subject and the object interact in the construction of physical knowledge. The idea of time is a reflection upon operations, but these operations are constrained by physical realities.

Piaget also considered the evolution of the notions of speed and force. The concept of force was important because particularly strong parallels exist between the development of the idea of force in history and the development of the same idea in the individual. Historically the development is characterized by decentration. For example, Aristotle's conception of force is egocentric, confusing subject and object, and it was superseded by the more decentered conception of classical mechanics. The concept becomes even more decentered in relativity theory, because it now applies to conditions not occurring on the scale of human activity. This developmental process parallels the progressive decentration that occurs in Piaget's stages of cognitive development.

Turning to the notions of conservation and object permanence, he again found laboriously constructed concepts. Conservation and object permanence, like other physical concepts, do not stem exclusively from either experience or rational deduction. Since the idea of object permanence denotes the physical invariant that subsists across physical transformations, it is the most basic of physical properties. In this context, the epistemology of sub-atomic physics took on particular importance for Piaget because there the concepts of object permanence, time, space, and causality acquire radically different meanings than they have in ordinary experience. Epistemological analysis may explain this phenomenon, since questions about the nature and limits of human knowledge appear when one reflects on the sub-atomic realm. In contrast, Piaget claimed that genetic epistemology resolved such paradoxes just as it accounted for the progressive constructions of mathematics.

He resolved the paradoxes of particle physics in the following way. As we have seen, the structures of physical knowledge result from the coordination of actions which are accommodated to the specific properties of physical objects. In other words, physical operatory structures apply to actions that can be performed physically on objects. This presupposes that actions can be differentiated from objects. At the level of microphysics, differentiation of actions and objects breaks down, since at that level entanglement occurs between the observer and the observed. In the sub-atomic universe, the concepts of causality, time, space, and object permanence no longer apply in the usual manner.

Most importantly, the epistemology of sub-atomic and relativity physics shows the indissociable relationship between the subject and the object of its knowledge. Normally, the effect of the subject upon the object—assimilation—and the effect of the object upon the subject—accommodation—go unnoticed. At the level of the cosmos and of particle physics, the interrelationship between the subject and object is more conspicuous. Thus he concluded that the interactionist conclusions of genetic epistemology fit the findings of contemporary physics. Paradoxes of time, posed by relativity theory, and of object permanence, posed by particle physics, are both elucidated by his interactionist model of knowledge.

The basic evolutionary tendencies of both mathematics and physics correspond with Piaget's assessment of the evolutionary process in the individual knower. Historical evolution of scientific concepts begins in a relative egocentrism. There the subject does not recognize the contributions of schemata to the appearance of reality and is unable to reflect upon the cognitive structures which construct this reality. Development is a process of decentering whereby the subject restructures previously constructed operations. Moreover, the process is one of an increasing awareness of the meaning of the subject's operations and the reality to which they apply. This basic evolutionary tendency is at work in the history of both mathematics and physics. From Plato and Aristotle to Descartes, Copernicus, Gödel, and Einstein, this reorientation of perspective and search for broader frames of reference manifests itself. The history of physics, like that of mathematics, provides evidence that Piaget's evolutionary model may be extended from the individual to the history of science. The history of both mathematics and physics supports the view that knowledge begins in interaction, extends the adaptation of the organism to its environment, and advances by reflective abstractions.

The Epistemology of Biology

Piaget opened his discussion of biological knowledge in volume three of *Introduction à l'épistémologie génétique* by comparing biological knowledge with the structure of mathematical and physical knowledge. Mathematics is idealistic, emphasizing both the assimilation of the object to the subject's schemata, and the activity of the subject in the construction of knowledge. Biology is realistic, accentuating both the accommodation of the subject's schemata to objects, and the role of the object in the construction of knowledge. Mathematics is characterized by deduction and inference, biology by experiment and observation. Physics stands between the two, assimilating reality to mathematical schemata and accommodating schemata to objects incapable of such assimilations.

Piaget began his remarks on the epistemology of biology, by noting that species and genera correspond to logical "groupings" of classes and relations. We saw in Chapter 1 that he believed in a connection between logic and biology but, unlike Aristotle, did not believe species and genera were categories of the natural world. Nevertheless, he did not agree with the nominalists that species and genera were purely arbitrary or conventional categories either. Piaget argued that the categories of genera and species result from assimilating biological reality to operatory schemata. In this way subjects actively construct their world without such constructions being arbitrary, since reality constrains those constructions. Thus, both the notion of species and the distinction between genotype and phenotype illustrate the way in which biological reality is assimilated to operatory schemata.

Next, Piaget noted that the Mendelian laws of inheritance have given biology a quantitative character. This might suggest that biology eventually will be reduced to mathematics; Piaget disagreed, since biological entities like species and genera have an evolutionary character. This makes them contingent upon relationships existing between the organism and the environment during the period they originated. As opposed to the necessity of logico-mathematical structures, the contingency of biological structures renders them incapable of complete assimilation to mathematical structures. The evolutionary character of biology raises an important issue for understanding Piaget's conception of evolution. Supposing knowledge proceeds towards a limit, does the evolution of life proceed toward a final end? Does any finality exist in the evolutionary process?

Piaget's discussion of finality began by considering vitalism as an explanation of evolutionary change. He agreed with vitalism's holism, but disagreed that totalities or vital forces explain evolution or that they exist independently of organisms. He rejected mechanism as well, since structural wholes are not reducible to their parts. Furthermore, he argued that finality does not direct evolution, and he reiterated that it is the "formation laws" governing evolutionary transformations that explain evolution. But do organisms proceed toward anything? Is there a specific conception of finality that is consistent with the evidence?

Piaget argued that the concept of finality parallels the concept of force in an important way. Just as the concept of force arises from the subjective impression of muscular effort, so too does the concept of finality arise from the subjective impression "that the goal of an action can constitute its cause."[21] The history of the notion of force in the physical sciences and of finality in the biological sciences reveals that the importance attached to these views has diminished. He attributed the decline in both notions to decentration, the gradual elimination of subjective and egocentric explanations. In this way, the evolution of biological explanations parallels the evolution of mathematical and physical ones and supports the extension of the evolutionary model from individuals to the scientific disciplines.

Piaget compared the belief in finality to hungry persons who believe that the goal of their appetite causes their action. This belief results from a confusion of physical and conscious states. Physiologically, hunger results from a temporary imbalance or disequilibrium in the organism, and a causal explanation according to equilibrium laws is sufficient to explain the activity aimed at reducing hunger. Psychologically, the physical state is translated into needs which confer value on the objects of the desires associated with those needs. These values then act as goals and actions become directed toward those goals until they are achieved. During this process needs are primary, since the relationship of means to ends is temporally unidirectional. That we can reverse this order and consider the end to direct the means only shows that consciousness is reversible. But the causes of action are the needs which initiate activity and the desire to achieve a state of equilibrium. Piaget concluded by arguing that the notion of finality, as causal agent directing the process of human evolution, confuses psychology and physiology.

> In conclusion, finality is only a system of implications between values attached to sensorimotor or representative anticipations, and final causes constitute an illusory notion resulting from the confusion between these psychological implications and the physiological series of causes. Objectively, or biologically, what one calls finality therefore corresponds to a march toward equilibrium.[22]

Notice that there is some direction implied in this conception of evolution because the invariant functions of the organism direct it toward equilibrium. But according to this notion of directionality there is no final destination to evolution. The belief in final causes results from confusing psychological implications and reversibility with the "march toward equilibrium." Piaget noted that the causal mechanisms involved in morphogenesis and embryogenesis resemble the workings of final causation, but he was quick to criticize a literal interpretation of these phenomena, especially when framed in the Aristotelian language as the transformation from potency to actuality.

> Just as psychological finality, as we saw earlier, simply translates in an unanalyzed way the passage from disequilibrium to equilib-rium ... in the same way the finalistic translation of the mechanisms of heredity or embryology as "potentialities" would in the same way signify nothing more than that one remains at the level of a global language for lack of grasping the detail of the transforma-tions themselves.[23]

The process can be explained without resorting to mysterious final causes working to actualize potentials. It is explained by equilibrium. Piaget exhorted us to give up teleology, and to search instead for laws governing the "detailed transformations."

He also spent a significant portion of the third volume reiterating the comparisons between theories of biological evolution and intel-lectual evolution. He thought these comparisons significant for two reasons. First, similar explanations in both biology and epistemology demonstrate the similarity of problems in both domains. Both study the history of forms whose genesis consists of successive adaptations between organism and environment. Second, such comparisons draw attention to the continuity between life and knowledge. Not only are there analogies between ontogenesis and the individual's psychogenesis, but more generally analogies exist between the evolution of organic reality and the evolution of knowledge. Life itself creates forms, including cognitive forms. Thus a continuity exists between life and knowledge which will be explained fully only when the laws govern-ing the transformation of forms are known. This continuity also reveals the place of biology in the circle of the sciences.

Biology thus proceeds from physico-chemistry but prepares psychology, and the biological theory of adaptation prepares epistemological solutions. It is without a doubt that one will in fact understand something precise about the mechanisms of knowledge when the day arrives where biology will have resolved the problem of the relation between the organism and the environment.[24]

Piaget's study of the history of science revealed an evolutionary process that parallels intellectual evolution in individuals. More importantly, he believed that the evidence adduced from the history of science justified the transfer of his analysis from the individual knower to the scientific disciplines. Essentially, the history of the sciences reveals the same progressive decentration as psychogenesis. The analysis of knowledge may be extended profitably from the part (the individual) to the whole (the history of science). This extension simply meant that Piaget came to believe that a phylogeny of reason closely parallels an ontogeny of reason. He now proceeded to draw his most general conclusions regarding this evolutionary process.

The Circle of the Sciences

In the conclusion of *Introduction à l'épistémologie génétique,* Piaget returned to the idea of the "circle of the sciences." Since genetic epistemology studies the growth of knowledge, and since the growth of knowledge in the various sciences had been considered, he was now in position to reflect upon the general lessons drawn from such an approach.[25]

The first lesson concerned the role played by the subject and the object in the construction of knowledge in the various sciences. Mathematics depends on the activity of the subject more than on objects, and is idealistic. Still, mathematical constructions agree with reality, revealing their "intrinsic objectivity." Physics is more realistic than mathematics. Physics investigates data exterior to the subject, but this exterior reality is not easily differentiated from the mathematical constructions that physics employs. Biology is the antithesis of mathematics since it investigates a historical process, and the data of biology is independent of the subject when compared with fields elaborated by mathematics. But biology studies organic reality which leads to the investigation of the evolution of knowledge in organic beings and, eventually, to psychology. The relationship between the subject and object in psychology is complex. On the one hand, the object of psychological knowledge is a subject. On the other hand, the subject can become an object of its own knowledge.

In a sense, the reduction of psychology to biology, physics, and, finally, mathematics and logic is possible. However, since logic and mathematics are explained by the psychological and physiological laws of the subject, they may be "reduced" to psychology. Thus, the sciences close in upon each other in the form of a circle that is characterized by the relationship between subjects and objects.

> Since all knowledge consists in an indissociable relationship between the subject and the object, such that the object is only known through its assimilation to the subject's activity and that the subject in return knows itself by the sole intermediary of its own actions, that is to say of its accommodations to the object, it is not surprising that this fundamental circle, inherent to the very act of knowing, is found again in the whole of knowledge that constitutes the total scientific system.[26]

This conclusion echoed the theme that knowledge at all levels involves an interaction of subject and object. Reality is known by its assimilation to subjects, and, at the same time, subjects are known to themselves by their accommodation to reality.

> Scientific thought is therefore oriented in two complementary directions: knowledge of the object, that is to say of exterior reality, by the means of this assimilation to the subject constituted by mathematics, while physics is so structured as to be destined to sooner or later absorb biology to the extent that this reduction will be possible; and knowledge of the subject, that is to say of living and mental organization, but by means of an inverse reduction from the subject to the object, carried out thanks to the physico-chemical methods of biology and to the organicist methods of psychology.

Psychology is itself split between these two tendencies: reduction of the subject to the object by its biological orientation and of the object to the subject by its effort at an operative explication of mathematical and physical ideas.[27]

In summary, mathematics reduces objects to subjects by assimilation, whereas biology reduces subjects to objects by accommodation. Physics and psychology stand between mathematics and biology. Physics reduces (assimilates) objects to the subject's mathematical schemata and reduces (accommodates) the subject to the objects of reality. Psychology reduces (assimilates) objects to the subject by explicating mathematics and reduces (accommodates) the subject to objects by biological explanations. The reduction of subjects to objects and objects to subjects are the two directions or orientations of scientific thinking. In effect, these two directions reveal why the circle of the sciences travels in either direction, and why the evolution of one science is bound to effect the others. The general conclusion to be drawn regarding the circle of the sciences is that it provides the framework in which the evolution of knowledge, as an interaction between subject and object, is possible.

Construction and Reflection

A major reason for the two directions of scientific thinking pertains to the fact that mathematics and physics consider the subject and object to be static, while in biology and psychology a developmental perspective dominates. This insight led Piaget to consider the developmental process. How is change to be understood? Piaget rejected Aristotle's view that A is preformed in B, a potentiality awaiting actualization. He likewise rejected the view that A and B bear no relationship to each other, since this would be to reject evolution. How then does knowledge grow? What is the relationship of successive theories in the history of science?

To answer this question, he returned again to the idea of "reflective abstraction." Since the growth of knowledge is not a mere accumulation of facts, the history of scientific interpretations answers questions about the growth of knowledge. Scientific knowledge grows: 1) a succession of constructions; and 2) reflections on those constructions. This relationship between construction and reflection is reciprocal because reflections are constructive, while at the same time constructions are based on reflections. "Every new construction, in 'reflecting' itself on the previous elements enriches them with properties that they did not possess by themselves."[28]

Reflective abstraction ensures both the novelty and the continuity of knowledge. Formal operational schemata are prepared by previous lower level schemata, preserving continuity with lower structures while, at the same time, surpassing them. Eventually this developmental continuity may be traced backward from formal to concrete operations, and then to sensorimotor behaviors, and finally the organic structure of the organism. This explains the process of evolutionary development without resorting to Aristotelian preformism or a non-developmental view. "Eventually the relation of the rational 'forms' and the organic 'forms' can thus be supported without preforming the former in the latter nor breaking genetic continuity at any point."[29]

Piaget had established, at least to his own satisfaction, that knowledge is a developmental process based upon construction and reflection. Moreover, the process works in both the ontogenesis and the phylogenesis of knowledge. But does this process have a direction?

The Growth of Knowledge as a Vector

Piaget commenced his discussion of the evolution of knowledge by rejecting a purely contingent explanation of it. The least we can say is that knowledge evolves as a "vector," that is, with some direction. To state the opposite implies that reason does not evolve rationally— that there is no reason for structural development. Since the growth of knowledge is no mere accumulation of facts, it has the directionality supplied by progressive re-equilibrations. The history of mathematics and physics provides ample evidence of this. The situation "thus compels us to only speak of a possible direction as relative to an operation immanent to reason and to an operation without a fixed structure."[30] And of course the vector or direction is the drive for equilibrium. "There is a vector, in intellectual evolution, to the extent that the change tends to retain the maximum possible from the past while integrating it in new forms . . . . The vector is therefore not anything other than the tendency towards equilibrium."[31]

The progressive integration of knowledge leads to more stable or equilibrated structures. Piaget reminded us that these progressive integrations do not destroy previous knowledge but absorb it in a greater synthesis. For instance, Euclidean geometry has been integrated into a higher (non-Euclidean) synthesis. The progress of knowledge entails both a conservation of the past and an integration of the novel. Even relativity theory and particle physics, which indicate major breaks with past theorizing, display this integration of the past and present.

The direction of the growth of knowledge is not characterized by formal logical principles for two reasons. First, because logical principles are themselves derivative from psychology, and second because what is contrary to reason changes. Piaget used the example of complementarity to explain the development of basic logical notions. Complementarity is a phenomenon in quantum mechanics where light has either wave or particle characteristics depending upon the context and both mutually exclusive (complementary) aspects are needed to understand light. Piaget believed this phenomenon presented grave problems for an axiomatic foundationalism. What he had in mind was that in terms of purely formal logic, the affirmation of contradictory predicates is paradoxical. This result suggested that formal principles do not direct the growth of knowledge but regulate its formalization.

He then argued that equilibration is more profound than formal principles and that the major criterion of all equilibrium is *reversibility*. Reversibility refers to the possibility of performing an action in a reverse direction. Logical principles like negation—not male equals female—and reciprocity—not better equals worse—are reversible. Reversibility also refers to the ability to perform simple logical operations. For example, a concrete operational child understands that an equivalent number of objects can be condensed or spread out without a change in the quantity of objects. If a row of pennies is spread out, the child knows that these changes can be annulled or negated. Intellectual coherence itself may be characterized by the ability to reverse operations; hence reversibility is prominent in characterizing successive scientific theories. In mathematics, for example, when a new theory includes its preceding one as an individual case, it is reversible in a certain sense. One understands the previous theory as a special case of the current one, or the current theory as a reflective abstraction from the previous one. Reversibility is also prominent in individual development, where the stages of development are characterized by an increasing reversibility of operations.

An important repercussion of this evolutionary view is that knowledge does not rest upon indubitable principles, whether they be logical, mathematical, or physical. Furthermore, knowledge and cognitive structures continually evolve but their final destination cannot be known. Yet we observe that the evolution of knowledge parallels that of individual development and both possess a directionality. Piaget summarized this evolutionary and directional view of human knowledge as follows: "In one word, reason does not evolve without reason and the evolution of its structures thus takes on, even though a posteriori, the look of a sort of orthogenesis."[32]

We may now summarize the main conclusions of the multi-volume *Introduction à l'épistémologie génétique*. Genetic epistemology in its general sense is the study of the direction inherent in the growth of knowledge. The demand for equilibrium supplies this direction (vector) and can be characterized as an orthogenesis toward a limit.[33] More than thirty years of research revealed that both psychogenesis and historiogenesis are orthogenetic—constituted by similar processes like decentration, reversibility, and reflective abstraction. The circle of the sciences provides a means by which this evolution can be understood, revealing the necessary interrelationship between the subject and the object in the constitution of knowledge. In short, the growth of knowledge derives from interactionism, extends organic functioning, aims at cognitive equilibrium, and is governed by the laws of cognitive evolution.

CHAPTER 4

The Final Position: Constructive Evolution

Piaget's publications in psychology alone during the 1960s and 1970s would have assured him great stature in psychology.[1] During this period, he also produced succinct summaries of his theory of developmental psychology in *The Psychology of the Child* (1966), his structuralism in *Structuralism* (1968), and his genetic epistemology in *The Principles of Genetic Epistemology* (1970). In addition to these multi-faceted investigations, he returned to the central problematic of his life's work—the relationship between biology and knowledge.

We may recall that Piaget's psychological investigations were a means of answering biological and epistemological questions simultaneously. By treating cognitive development as a kind of mental embryogenesis, he could draw comparisons between cognitive and biological development. This would allow him to construct a biological theory of knowledge and a conception of evolution applicable to both biology and epistemology. *Biology and Knowledge: An Essay on the Relations Between Organic Regulations and Cognitive Processes* (1971), introduced his biological theory of knowledge and a new theory of biological evolution. It also effected a synthesis of his biological, psychological, and epistemological theorizing; a synthesis further elaborated in *Adaptation and Intelligence* (1974) and *Behavior and Evolution* (1976).

Biology and Knowledge

Auto-regulation in Biology and Knowledge

Piaget's biological approach to knowledge had been evident in his earliest writings. The idea that there are common principles of organization operating in both biological and cognitive development was already present in *Recherche*, and much of *Biology and Knowledge* was devoted to explicating these common principles. According to this account of development, knowledge is the progressive adaptation of the organism to the environment, whether of a snail reconstructing its shape or of a child its actions and ideas. During this ongoing organism/environment interaction, the organism goes through a series of stages which are characterized by structures or forms of organization which tend toward equilibrium. The process by which successive equilibrium states are reached is called *equilibration*. This process is the essence of both biological and cognitive functioning— providing the link between biology and knowledge.

In addition to equilibration, Piaget argued that other factors influence development: maturation, experience, and social transmission.[2] These factors are the necessary but not sufficient conditions for development. Knowledge does not result exclusively from maturation, since children attain levels of cognitive development at various ages. Experience of physical reality is insufficient to explain knowledge because many concepts arising at the concrete level cannot be derived from experience. And social transmission is not sufficient either because it cannot explain the increase of knowledge over time. The most important factor in development is equilibration, the process which underlies the genesis of new biological and cognitive forms. As evidence for the existence of equilibration, Piaget compared biological and cognitive functioning.

At the start of *Biology and Knowledge*, Piaget affirmed the continuity between intellectual epigenesis and "embryological epigenesis and the organic formation of phenotypes."[3] The basic reason for this continuity is that both cognitive and biological evolution raise the problem of the relationship of organism, specifically the genome, and the environment. These remarks set the stage for the major theme of the work: "Life is essentially autoregulation."[4] Self or *autoregulation* is a universal characteristic of life, and the basis of behavior from the simplest forms of organic regulations to the most complex forms of scientific and mathematical thinking. "Every living organization, at every level of evolution, contains autoregulations, and the same thing applies, a fortiori, I would say, in the field of behavior."[5] Autoregulations are the basis of the cognitive processes which regulate the organism. In the case of humans, cognitive processes are the primary means of interacting with the environment.

> Cognitive processes seem, then, to be at one and the same time the outcome of organic autoregulation, reflecting its essential mechanisms, and the most highly differentiated organs of this regulation at the core of interactions with the environment, so much so that, in the case of man, these processes are being extended to the universe itself.[6]

Autoregulation is the process by which living things become equilibrated; hence, it is synonymous with equilibration. Equilibration/autoregulation is one of three factors governing organic growth noted in *Biology and Knowledge*, the others being programming by the genome and environmental influence. This restates his earlier view, namely that genetic programming corresponds to maturation and environmental influence to physical knowledge and social transmission. Piaget granted hereditary and environmental factors in development but insisted that they are not sufficient to explain development. Heredity and environment do not account for the necessity of equilibration/autoregulation—the universal proclivity toward stable relationships between the organism and environment, and the propensity to create new forms to achieve that objective. This insight, that neither genome nor environment is sufficient to account for development, is the basis for Piaget's rejection of both Lamarckism and Darwinism.

Methodology: Comparing Biology and Knowledge

Having stated that the major problem is to uncover the commonalities between organic and cognitive autoregulation, Piaget discussed the methods with which the investigation was to proceed. On the one hand, the method would not consist of reducing biology to cognition by projecting characteristics of intelligence or intentionality into biology. On the other hand, it would not reduce cognition to biology by equating cognitive processes with organic ones. Cognition extends biological functioning; in other words, surpasses physiology qualitatively. This implies that biology and cognition, although formally analogous, are not identical. Since biology and knowledge cannot be reduced to each other, the method for uncovering their similarities involves extensive comparisons between the two.

> One initial method of approach, although it can hardly be said to have any built-in control, is to bring out the close relationship between cognitive and biological problems. We have already seen this in the case of the epigenesis of intelligence and ontogenetic development of an organic nature, but this is merely a particular instance, and the method to be followed in comparing the main problems is a much more general one. The method underlying this general form is to list the problems common to biological studies and psychological research into cognitive functions or scientific epistemology. Now, in any attempt to set up such a list it immediately becomes apparent that these common problems are either of an entirely local or of the most general kind—the kind, in fact, which is bound to recur at every important juncture in the study of biology.[7]

Piaget was not concerned with the "local problems." These refer to specific connections between acts of perception and the nervous system, intelligence and physiology, or instinct and neurology. He was interested in the more general ones.

As for the general problems which are our main concern in this work, it is impossible to formulate them without at once being struck by the close connection between vital mechanisms and cognitive ones. All knowledge, in fact, of whatever nature it may be, raises the problem of the relations between the subject and the object, and this problem can lead to many solutions according to whether one attributes such knowledge to the subject alone, to an action by the object, or to the interactions of both. Now, since the subject is one aspect of the organism, and the object a sector, as it were, of the environment, the problem of knowledge, seen from this point of view, corresponds to the problem of the relations between the organism and its environment—undeniably the most general question in the whole of biology.[8]

Here Piaget stated a theme that persists throughout his works: that the most general biological questions have their parallels in epistemology. Not only are there similarities between the problems of biology and epistemology, there are also functional connections, structural isomorphisms, and comparative models that connect the two spheres. In addition, we can compare human and sub-human intelligence. Piaget was impressed with Lorenz' work in ethology and quoted Darwin to the effect that understanding animals will make significant contributions to epistemology. Finally, one must apply explicative theories of biology to understanding cognitive functioning, particularly logico-mathematical structures and their correspondence with reality. What biological theory of adaptation best explains this correspondence? The entire purpose of the book is to explain the adaptation of mind/organism to object/environment.

The rejection of reductionism provided Piaget the opportunity to present the clearest account of his methodology. His argument for a biologically based epistemology, and a theory of evolution applicable to both biology and epistemology, would rest upon the similarities and differences between the two domains. His entire project explained knowledge by analogies to biology, and his enterprise should be evaluated on that ground. Notice that despite his belief that a theory of evolution applies to both areas, he did not presuppose that there is a parallel between the two. To establish the parallel he had to present the evidence for a biologically based epistemology. Notice also that the similarities between the two domains are a necessary but not sufficient condition for the applicability of an evolutionary account of both.

Having determined the problems to be discussed and the methods to be followed, Piaget turned to the epistemology of biological knowledge. The nature of biological knowledge is important because of what it reveals about the nature of the subject who constructs this knowledge. Since the subject and the object of its knowledge exist interdependently, knowledge of one illuminates the nature of the other.

The Epistemology of Biological Knowledge

Piaget began his discussion of biological knowledge by distinguishing between its diachronic and synchronic dimensions. The diachronic dimension concerns the dynamic aspects of biology—development and evolution—while the synchronic dimension concerns the static aspects—organization and physiology.

Turning first to the synchronic concepts in biology, he considered the notion of species as central to understanding the character of states of equilibrium. He noted that Aristotelian and creationist notions of species were realist; that is, they considered species immutable, existing independently of individuals. Lamarckians are nominalists because they consider species to be temporary, conventional, and mind dependent. As opposed to both conceptions, Piaget believed that contemporary biology was moving toward a third notion of species, where species are relational totalities sharing a genetic pool. The various conceptions of species can be clarified by considering various conceptions of society in the social sciences. Society can be said to exist: 1) on its own, over and above individuals (realist); 2) as merely a collection of individuals (nominalist); or 3) as the totality of the relations between individuals and society (relationalism or interactionism).

Turning to the diachronic dimension, Piaget traced various conceptions of evolution from Aristotle to contemporary biology. Aristotle distinguished biological forms—vegetative, sensitive, and rational—

but he did not see them as evolving from each other. Creationist theories are non-evolutionary since they see forms as timeless entities that carry out a pre-established plan. Many neo-Darwinians and modern geneticists insist that the genome contains all of the possibilities that will be realized in the genesis of the individual. Piaget opposed this genetic "preformism," maintaining instead that evolution is "constructive." According to this view, new possibilities emerge as the system moves from one state of equilibrium to another. Piaget was well aware that this constructive aspect of his theory had much in common with the Hegelian dialectic and the important Hegelian notion of *aufgehoben*. Piaget also pointed out that this conception of evolution applied to the evolution of cognition. While this may appear obvious, the idea that reason evolves has been opposed by most of the great philosophers, from Plato to Aristotle, Descartes, Leibniz, and Kant. Piaget's detailed observations over many decades convinced him that these philosophers were mistaken, and that both mind and body evolve.

> Thus, the idea eventually caught on . . . that reason itself is not an absolute invariable but is elaborated through a series of creative operational constructions, which introduce new features and are preceded by an uninterrupted series of preoperational constructions. These result from coordinations of actions and can be traced right back to morphogenetic organization and to biological organization in general.[9]

This conception of the evolutionary process is supported by the evidence accumulated from four fields of study: individual psychogenesis, the history of science, ethology, and genetics. Piaget's own work had focused on the first two fields, but he also believed that contemporary biology was adopting a similar conception of evolution. Fundamentally, this conception describes an epigenetic process resulting from the continual interaction of organism and environment. Piaget believed that contemporary theories were moving away from a total emphasis on random changes in the genome toward various types of interactionism. He did not believe that the phenotype was entirely predetermined in the genotype, but that biological evolution proceeds through a series of "epigentic" exchanges. Again he rejected biological preformism and affirmed biological interactionism.

Piaget presented his version of evolution as an alternative to Lamarckism and Darwinism. It was an evolutionary theory which did not emphasize either the environment or the organism as the source of evolutionary change. In other words, a theory that emphasized neither endogenous variations subsequently selected by the environment nor exogenous factors leading to hereditary fixation. An exponent of this alternative was C.H. Waddington, and Piaget interpreted Waddington's position as emphasizing: 1) the totality of relations among the structures of the organism, i.e., the genotype and phenotype, and 2) the interaction of the organism and the environment. This interactionist biology closely paralleled Piaget's findings in psychology and epistemology. If this theory were correct, Piaget's theory of evolution could be justifiably extended profitably from psychology and the epistemology of the sciences to biology. It would also vindicate his belief that laws of form operate at multiple levels of reality.

Additional support for the belief that laws of form operate at various levels of reality was provided by the isomorphisms drawn between functions and structures in both biology and cognition. Piaget used the term "functioning" to refer to the activity of structures. He distinguished between "specialized functions," the activity of a sub-structure on the total structure, and the general "organization function," the activity of the whole exerted on the parts or sub-structures. The properties of the general organizational function—conservation of form, differentiation of parts, and continual self-renewal—are the universal conditions of living organisms, and they apply at all levels of organization. In essence, this restated his belief that life is essentially autoregulation and reiterated his position in *The Origins of Intelligence in Children* that organization and adaptation are functional invariants applying at multiple levels of reality. The parallels between biological and cognitive functioning support the view that universal laws of organization govern both biological and cognitive evolution.

A Biological Interpretation of Knowledge

Much of *Biology and Knowledge* explicated how the laws of organization manifest themselves at various levels of biological functioning: in the nervous system and reflexes, in instinctive behaviors and perception, and in the earliest types of learning and behavior. The continuity between biological organization and knowledge suggests that there are three basic types of knowledge: instinctive or inherited, logico-mathematical, and acquired knowledge.

Instinctive knowledge is important because of its close proximity with biological functioning. Piaget asserted that instinctive knowing results when environmental disequilibrium initiates a non-specific message to the genetic system. Assuming that equilibrium results at the genetic level as a response to the disequilibrium, the genetic structural change is inherited by subsequent generations. This conception of evolution does affirm that information is transmitted from the environment to the genetic pool. However, Piaget claimed that this was not Lamarckism because the habits or behaviors associated with instinctive knowing are not directly transmitted to future generations. There is no "imprint" of environment on the organism; rather, the genome responds to disequilibrium at the phenotypic level with directed variations at the genotypic level and some of these variations are then selected by the environment. The endogenous structures of the organism react to the disequilibrium caused by the environment.

It is important to realize that the organism is active in this process of responding to the environment, that is, it does not merely accept or "copy" the changes at the level of the phenotype. Instead, the activity of the organism is directed and thus the theory differs markedly from the "chance" mutations that occur according to the neo-Darwinians. Evolution does not proceed exclusively by chance genetic recombinations, by environmental pressure on the genome, nor by any biological preformism. Rather, it involves new constructions which are directed in response to organism/environment interaction. Piaget alluded to the work of many contemporary biologists as providing at least partial support for his claim.[10] (Note the emphasis on the accessibility of the genome with respect to its environment.) This biological interactionism is reminiscent of Piaget's psychological and epistemological inter-actionism. Instinctive knowledge evolves from this interaction, and he offered his biological research as evidence for his theory.

Piaget also repeated much of what has been previously discussed regarding mathematical knowledge. Mathematical knowledge is nei-ther a learned or exogenous activity nor does it result exclusively from maturation or heredity. Rather it is an endogenous construction where actions are internalized and organized as operatory structures. Ac-quired or physical knowledge is exogenous since it results from the organism's adaptation to the environment. Physical knowledge is connected with logico-mathematical knowledge for two reasons. First, logico-mathematical knowledge, though derived from coordi-nations of actions, is directed toward objects since actions usually apply to objects. In this sense, even pure mathematics is related to objects. Second, physical reality must be represented by a mathemati-cal framework, especially when this reality is beyond our normal perceptions, for instance, at the sub-atomic level. This is because elaborate knowledge of physical reality—the kind derived from experiment—is not amenable to a hereditary framework.

In summary, innate knowledge is fundamentally phenotypic adaptation in concert with genotypic structures. Acquired knowledge is phenotypic adaptation in concert with mathematical structures. Logico-mathematical knowledge transcends both innate knowing and acquired knowledge, but it is one case of the adaptation of mind/organism to reality/environment. At the level of innate knowledge, cognition is only partially differentiated from organic regulations. At the level of logico-mathematical knowledge, cognition becomes increasingly differentiated from them. The continuity between bio-logical and cognitive functioning justifies the extension of the model of evolution from biology to epistemology and back again, demon-strating the way in which the sciences are intertwined.

Perhaps the most important result of *Biology and Knowledge* was placing knowledge within an evolutionary perspective that is neither neo-Lamarckian nor neo-Darwinian. He also reasserted his belief that knowledge results from an interaction of the organism and environ-ment by characterizing the organism as an "open system" in its exchanges with the environment. The organism extends itself toward the environment, while simultaneously attempting to conserve its own organization. Knowledge is the evolutionary adaptation that fulfills both of these functions, since it assimilates the environment at the same time it tends toward stable equilibrium. The drive toward equilibrium gives rise to the new forms of organization that characterize evolution. Biological organization, since it continually transcends itself, is the source of both evolutionary adaptation and knowledge. This is the sense in which knowledge is essentially a construction. Piaget believed that he had justified his two main theses: cognition extends organic regulations and regulates exchanges with the environment.

Behavior: The Motor of Evolution

The Theory of the Phenocopy

In addition to presenting his biological view of knowledge, a central idea in *Biology and Knowledge* was that phenotypic adaptation can bring about genotypic restructuring. In *Adaptation and Intelligence*, Piaget answered those critics who interpreted this idea as Lamarckian, and he attempted to specify situations in which phenotypic adaptation could become hereditarily fixed. He did this by positing a middle way between Lamarck and Darwin. Lamarck had overemphasized the phenotype and environment as causal agents in evolution, while Darwin had placed too much emphasis with the genotype and heredity. Piaget argued that biological adaptation, like its cognitive counterpart, results from organism/environment interaction.

We begin with a brief recapitulation of the biological evidence upon which this theory is based. We may recall that the pond snail, *Limnaea stagnalis,* adapts to turbulent waters by shortening its shell. Piaget demonstrated that this phenotypic adaptation became hereditarily fixed by moving the *Limnaea* to still waters where their globular (shortened) shape remained. However, the phenotypic adaptation of snails who shortened their shells when placed in aquariums with agitators designed to simulate turbulent waters, quickly reverted to the elongated shape when returned to still waters. Neo-Darwinism claims that the globular shells result from random mutations subsequently selected by the environment. According to this explanation, the globular shell is not found in still waters because those environments select against it. However, when Piaget placed this variety in still waters he found that they survived quite well. If random mutations accounted for this phenomenon, one would expect globular snails to be randomly distributed. Why then was the globular variety found exclusively in turbulent waters? Piaget hypothesized that the phenomenon was due to phenotypic adaptation followed by genetic mutation. This reversed the neo-Darwinian view that genotypes precede phenotypes.

He encountered similar results with the plant genus *Sedum*. A particular variety, *Sedum parvulum*, exhibited distinctive features as a response to harsh environmental conditions. In some species of *Sedum* these features exist as non-hereditary adaptations, because the plants revert to their usual form when transplanted to normal environments. In the *Sedum parvulum* these features were hereditarily fixed, since their distinctive features remain when transplanted to different environments. In the case of hereditary fixation, new genotypes replaced phenotypic adaptations. This was true in the *parvulum*, just as it had been in the *Limnaea stagnalis*.[11]

In order to explain how phenotypic adaptation leads to genotypic restructuring, Piaget redefined the notion of phenocopy to refer to a genotype that copies a phenotype. He was careful to distinguish his interpretation of phenocopy from Lamarckism. His theory, as opposed to Lamarck's, recognized that acquired characteristics are not always inherited and that the organism is not passive with respect to the environment.

The essence of Piaget's model of phenocopy may be summarized as follows. First, the organism responds to a change in the external environment with a somatic (pertaining to the body) modification. If this modification does not cause disequilibrium, the phenotypic adaptation does not become hereditarily fixed. Second, if there is disequilibrium between the exogenous modification and the endogenous hereditary program, then disequilibrium is "transmitted" to the internal environment. Third, if epigenetic development cannot re-establish equilibrium, the disequilibrium may descend all the way to the genome. Fourth, at the level of the genome, mutations respond to disequilibrium. The response of the genome is random in the sense that mutations do not necessarily restore equilibrium, but they are directed toward the needs of the organism. Fifth, the endogenous variations are then selected by both the internal and external environments until stability is restored. And finally, these variations result in endogenous reconstruction, i.e., they become hereditarily fixed. We may note a significant similarity between genomic and cognitive variations; both are directed toward responding to the needs of the organism.

The distinctive feature of this model is the way in which the phenotype and genotype interact. Not only do changes in DNA, cells, and tissues ultimately effect the organism's body and behavior, but the reverse is equally true. He supported this belief, that non-specific messages are sent back to the genome, with evidence from molecular genetics which suggests that information can move from RNA back to DNA. The model also explained why the genotype does not always copy the phenotype. It copies a phenotype only if the disturbance at the phenotypic level is sufficient to cause disequilibrium at the level of the genome. Since evolution results from interactionism, both the organism's passive reception of the environment and random genetic mutations are rejected as the sole causal agents of evolution. In this sense biological evolution, like cognitive development, is a constructive process.

> It is worth emphasizing, finally, that this interpretation of the phenocopy is basically constructivist in nature. The new genotype constitutes the ultimate result of conflicts and interactions between organism and environment, and the environment thus necessarily intervenes as one of the transforming elements in its causality. If this is so (and here lies the constructivism), then the adaptation itself has, as its producing factor, not the environment as such, but rather the constant action of the organism on the environment, which is by no means the same thing.[12]

Evolution is a construction, since the organism's action provides much of the impetus for evolutionary change and new forms depend upon which constructed variations are selected. This process explains why evolution is "open" regarding the future, that is, dependent upon past, present, and future constructions.

> The notion of any "totality of possibilities" then becomes a paradox because the realization of any one possibility will open up new ones. It is precisely this opening up, . . . which constitutes evolutionary progress.[13]

Piaget believed that the theory of the phenocopy had a cognitive equivalent. In cognition, exogenous knowledge is defined as deriving from physical experience and endogenous knowledge as deriving from logico-mathematical construction. The cognitive equivalent of phenocopy consists in replacing physical knowledge with logico-mathematical knowledge. This replacement does not merely copy reality because reality does not display the universality and necessity of logic and mathematics. Replacement involves generalization and reconstruction of the phenomenon experienced. Yet Piaget noted a dissimilarity between cognitive and biological phenocopy; cognitive disequilibrium need not extend back to the genome.

He explained this dissimilarity by returning to the two types of abstraction. Empirical abstraction is the source of exogenous knowledge and parallels phenotypic variations. Reflective abstraction is the source of endogenous knowledge and is reminiscent of the genotype. But reflective abstraction, as the source of cognitive forms, differs from the genotype in two ways. First, the abstract endogenous structures that originate in reflective abstraction escape programming from the genome. They develop because of the self-regulating mechanisms constitutive of equilibration. Though this process has its ultimate source in biology, it is not directly related to heredity. Second, reflective abstraction frees form from content. Genotypes, on the other hand, are always embodied in phenotypes.

These dissimilarities appear problematic for Piaget, yet he turned them to his advantage. On the one hand, he asserted the continuity between reflective abstraction and biology. On the other hand, higher level abstractions have "escaped" biology, specifically genetic programming, by freeing form from content. This reaffirmed the view that reflective abstraction extends organic functioning at the same time it transcends it. Still, these abstractions turn out to apply to nature, even predicting what will be found in nature. In this sense, the disanalogies between biological activity, represented by the interaction of phenotype and genotype, and cognitive activity, represented by the replacement of exogenous with endogenous knowledge, support his claim that the latter derives from the former while surpassing it.

The most salient similarity between biological and cognitive evolution is that both are constructive processes involving a directedness due to the demand of the system for equilibrium. Piaget introduced the term "maximizing equilibrium" to refer to the tendency of the organism "not simply to return to the former state, but to go beyond it in the direction of the best possible equilibrium compatible with the situation."[14] He also compared his equilibration theory with contemporary theories of self-organizing systems. Equilibration is the process by which living systems become increasingly organized; living systems are self-organizing systems.

Piaget's entire evolutionary biology disputed neo-Darwinism. He compared the neo-Darwinian view that chance mutations cause evolutionary change, to supposing that "the apple which chanced to fall beside Newton was the source of the great man's theories of gravitation."[15] He argued that Newton's genius resulted from a constructive process of hereditary and environmental interaction, and a long history of reflective abstractions. "Newton struggled to attain the prior conditions which were not random and were even necessary for his apparently aleatory inventions."[16]

From his earlier studies, Piaget believed that the evolution of knowledge resulted from the subject's internalization and reconstruction of the objects of knowledge. Analogously, he believed that his biological experimentation demonstrated that morphogenesis resulted from phenocopy, the internalization of aspects of the environment. Between construction of biological form and the construction of human knowledge lie an intermediate realm, the realm of behavior.

A Phenocopy of Behavior

Piaget's evolutionary biology placed an increasing importance on the "constant action of the organism on the environment," in other words, on the organism's behavior. He defined behavior in the first sentence of *Behavior and Evolution* as "action directed by organisms toward the outside world in order to change conditions therein or to change their own situation in relation to these surroundings."[17] Behavior includes sensorimotor activity, animal and plant reflexes, and human intelligence. However, it excludes internal activity like muscle contraction, blood circulation, and respiration. Behavior is distinguished from the latter activities because it aims at transforming or utilizing the external environment.

In *Behavior and Evolution*, Piaget hypothesized that behavior is the most significant determinant of evolution. He mentioned that this was not a new or radical hypothesis, and that modern ethology supported it. But how does one conceptualize the relationship between behavior and evolution? Lamarck assumed that behavior is the source of evolutionary variations, since acquired characteristics are inherited. Darwin, on the contrary, assumed that behavior played no significant role in evolution because genetic mutations are the source of evolutionary variations. According to the Neo-Darwinians behavior is not the cause of evolution; it is the effect. But if genetic variations are isolated from behavior, how do we explain the organism's adaptation to the world? Piaget found the neo-Darwinian answer—that adaptation results from a long process of fortuitous mutations—unacceptable.

His own theory of the phenocopy was one possible way to account for the role of behavior in evolution. He compared his own theory with those of the psychologist J.M. Baldwin, the biologist C.H. Waddington, and the neurobiologist Paul Weiss. All of these theorists argued that the organism's activity influences evolution. This activity was construed variously as reacting to, accommodating to, or choosing the environment. The goal of *Behavior and Evolution* was to examine the possible role behavior played in evolution. Whether one construed behavior as the product of genetic variation, or as the producer of evolutionary change, there can be no doubt that the two are inextricably linked. This restated Piaget's belief that biology is concerned with the relationship between endogenous change and exogenous activity.

Adaptational behavior not only facilitates survival, Piaget argued, it also expands both the habitable and, ultimately, the knowable environments. Furthermore, in the process of expanding its environment, the organism restructures it. Because some endogenous variations must respond to the organism's need to expand and restructure its environment, chance is an unlikely source of variation. In this context, the relationship between endogenous variations and exogenous activity is the central issue to be resolved. He proceeded to discuss various characterizations of this relationship.

Having found something of value in the theories of Baldwin, Waddington, and Weiss, Piaget advanced his own theory of behavior's role in evolution. According to his theory, the phenocopy mediates between adaptive behavior and the genotype in evolutionary transformations. We have already discussed the role phenocopy plays in the hereditary fixation of morphological traits but Piaget also examined the theory in the context of behavior. He cited Lorenz' work with ducks, in order to show how phenotypical behaviors can become hereditarily fixed. Whether we speak of phenocopy regarding morphological or behavioral traits, the process is one whereby the organism's activity modifies the genome. Piaget noted that not all behavior results in genotypic alteration, for example, human language is not inherited. This led him to believe that between non-inherited and inherited behavior exist many intermediate categories.

He also proposed the following account of the interaction between the organism's behavior and the genome. The process begins when the organism responds to a prolonged change in the environment with a new or modified behavior. If the new behavior results in internal disequilibrium, the disequilibrium is communicated to the genome. Piaget made it clear that the message is non-specific—"something is not functioning normally"—and he appealed to Weiss' observation that genes are not isolated but interact with higher levels of organized systems to support his claim. The genome responds to disequilibrium by "trying out" new variations. This process is not random, since the variations respond to the organism's needs, but it is not pre-programmed either, inasmuch as it may take many variations for the genome to respond properly. These variations are then selected by the internal environment with the purpose of restoring equilibrium between the genome and the internal environment. Because the internal environment has been modified by new behaviors that embody the external environment, and inasmuch as the genic variations must "fit" the internal environment, there is a convergence between the new genotype and the phenotypical behavior. Notice that the new phenotype does not become fixated in the genome, as the Lamarckians claimed, but that endogenous construction brings about an equilibrium between endogenous and exogenous forces. Whereas the neo-Darwinians claimed this construction is random, Piaget claimed it is partially directed. The phenocopy supplies the internal environment with information about the external environment and accounts for behavioral or morphological adaptation.

Behavior: The Motor of Evolution

Piaget had maintained that the organism is an "open" system in exchange with the environment. The behavior of an organism accommodates to, acts upon, interacts with, and restructures its environment. This realization led Piaget to affirm the major thesis of the work. "It is of the essence of behavior that it is forever attempting to transcend itself and that it thus supplies evolution with its principle motor."[18]

Again, Piaget offered this thesis in contradistinction to neo-Darwinism. He argued persuasively that physico-chemical transformations do not cause the extraordinary increase in complexity that characterizes higher organisms. The reason is that physiologically, the organism's basic characteristic is conservation, rather than change and mutation, and well-adapted organisms have no reason to change. It thus appears that evolutionary causation is found in the relationship between the organism's openness to the environment and its organizational propensities. Behavior innovatively responds to environmental obstacles by organizing and adapting to them, and it strives to improve itself, extend itself, and increase control over the environment.

In describing the process by which behavior responds innovatively to environmental stimulus, Piaget returned to the notions of assimilation and accommodation. He made an important distinction between physiological assimilation, which repeatedly incorporates substances or energies into the organism, and behavioral assimilation, which extends itself by the memory of past actions. Thus, the former is characterized by repetition, the latter by extension or transcendence. Physiological and behavioral accommodations are also distinguished in that the former are merely passive replacements that abolish preexisting structures, whereas the latter actively refine and integrate previous behavioral schemata. These distinctions reveal that behavior has a capacity for change that physiology lacks.

> In short, when we compare the basic functional mechanisms common to physiology and behavior, we find a systematic contrast between the conservative tendencies which predominate in the physiological realm and the expansionist factors which in the realm of behavior push assimilation and accommodation combined toward what appears to constitute behavior's dual goal on all levels: to widen the environment and to increase the living organism's capacities.[19]

Physiologically, primitive organisms are as well adapted as higher ones, but, behaviorally, there is a great disparity between lower and higher organisms. Behavior in vertebrates, most notably their insatiable curiosity, opposes the conservative proclivities of physiology. It continually seeks to transcend itself and favors the construction of new behavioral schemata. Still, this provides no assurance that behavior is the motor of evolution for behavior may be dependent on the nervous system. In response to this objection, Piaget cited evidence that behavior plays a role in the formation of the nervous systems much as the reverse.

These considerations allowed him to reaffirm his thesis that great evolutionary transformations cannot be explained solely by chance mutations. Consider the two alternatives. Either the organism's structure and behavior evolve independently, both resulting from chance occurrences which are later selected by the environment, or morphology and behavior are coordinated in the evolutionary process. If the latter is the case, then behavior is the motor of evolution because it mediates between the organism and environment and, by its nature, tends to supersede itself. The choice between these conceptual models is striking.

> In sum, either chance and selection can explain everything or else behavior is the motor of evolution. The choice is between an alarming waste in the shape of multitudinous and fruitless trials preceding any success no matter how modest, and a dynamics with an internal logic deriving from those general characteristics of organization and self-regulation peculiar to all living things."[20]

Here the contrast between a rational and a random evolution is apparent. While Piaget's affirmation of a logical and law-governed process is problematic, the neo-Darwinians must account for the biological and cognitive functioning of higher vertebrates by a process that is fundamentally irrational. Given the alternatives, Piaget's solution is appealing. We should note that he did not deny that some evolutionary variations, particularly morphological ones, are the outcome of chance. But he argued that behavior, say nest-building in birds, could not be explained in this way. Can one suppose that inept birds built frail, conspicuous nests until mutations produced more skillful nest-builders? Piaget believed this position—that evolution results from chance alone—absurd and supported his contention by pointing to particular differences between behavioral and mutational adaptation.

In the first place, behavior is teleonomic.[21] Whereas mutations are random and generated independent of the environment, behavior is goal oriented and aims at reshaping the environment. Mutations promote survival, sturdiness, and reproductive capacity, while behavioral adaptations are judged according to their success in fulfilling a purpose. Finally, the "fit" or correlation between behavior and the environment depends upon the behavioral phenocopy. The distinctions between behavioral and ordinary variations show why behavior is the most significant factor in the evolutionary process.

> This is why, in contrast to the conservative tendencies characterizing the internal organization of living things, behavior must be deemed the principal factor in evolution. To the extent that evolutionary "progress" depends at once on the growth of the power of organisms over their environment and on the relative independence they acquire as a result of their actions . . . behavior must be considered the motor of all these transformations. And no matter how neurological, physiological, or even biochemical the preconditions of behavior may be, the fact remains that behavior itself creates those higher unitary activities without which macro-evolution would be incomprehensible.[22]

Piaget concluded *Behavior and Evolution* by recognizing some distinctions between *variational* and *organizing* evolution. Variational evolution is random, takes place primarily at the genetic level, and is subject to a posteriori selection. In contrast, organizing evolution is teleonomic. It effects the entire organism and strives to establish a rapport or equilibrium between the organism and the environment. Organizing evolution brings about new behavioral forms and the organs that serve them as behavioral instruments. Selection results from an equilibrium achieved between the internal and epigenetic environments and phenotypic traits. Piaget claimed that genetic reconstruction of learned behavior in no way implied a return to Lamarckism, inasmuch as the internal environment selects the hereditary variations that respond to the organism's needs. In other words, it is not the action of the environment but action by the organism on the environment that stimulates the internal change to which variations respond. Future advances in genetics may result from reconciling the two types of evolution, necessitating a reconciliation of the discrete units that are subject to variational evolution, and the overall dynamic organization characteristic of all living things. *Behavior and Evolution* reached two admittedly speculative conclusions. "The first is that there is an organizing evolution as well as a variational one; and the second is that behavior is its motor."[23]

The emphasis on behavior and the theory of the phenocopy concluded Piaget's evolutionary theorizing. Behavior, as opposed to biochemical transformation, moves evolution in the direction of increasing autoregulation. Piaget's next task was to determine if his conception of constructive evolution resolves the most pressing issue for the belief in the evolution of knowledge: the problem of scientific change. The application of Piaget's model to an issue under debate at the epistemological level serves as a test case for the value of his conception of evolution.

CHAPTER 5

Psychogenesis and the History of Science:
Piaget and the Problem of Scientific Change

As we have seen, Piaget argued that his evolutionary model could be profitably extended from psychogenesis to the history of the sciences. Thus, his conception of evolution provides a possible solution to the problem of scientific change—the problem of whether an epistemology can account for the emergence of new scientific theories and simultaneously avoid historical relativism. Contemporary philosophy of science is largely concerned with the issue of how science moves from one theory to another and whether such change is justified. The application of his theory to this problem serves as a test case for the value of his approach and, moreover, resolving this fundamental issue in the philosophy of science enhances the theory. To better situate Piaget's resolution to the problem of scientific change, we will briefly summarize Thomas Kuhn's influential theory of scientific change. We will then consider how Piaget's theory responds to specific aspects of Kuhn's challenge.

Kuhn's Model of Scientific Change

Paradigms and Normal Science

In *The Structure of Scientific Revolutions*, Thomas Kuhn argues that science changes through a series of revolutionary *paradigm shifts*, where paradigms are "universally recognized scientific achievements that for a time provide model problems and solutions to a community of practitioners."[1] Before the emergence of paradigms, a pre-scientific stage exists in which observations, conjectures, and hypotheses cannot be assimilated into a coherent framework. Subsequently, the early development of most sciences is characterized by competition between a number of distinct but unconfirmed theories.

Eventually a virtual consensus emerges regarding a particular paradigm. That paradigm then determines which experiments are worth performing and what data is relevant. In short, paradigms determine the course of scientific research and provide the conceptual framework within which normal science is conducted. Normal science is activity which articulates and refines the paradigm; it does not put forth new paradigms. Thus, paradigms are relatively stable, and, within the confines of a paradigm, scientists function as "puzzle-solvers" who resolve particular puzzles as they arise. But if paradigms limit one's perspective by subsuming divergent facts into their framework, what initiates a paradigm shift?

Crisis and Revolution

It is the appearance of problems or anomalies that precipitates a crisis for the existing paradigm. If the old paradigm cannot be modified to account for new data and observations, new models are proposed. The resulting state is one of crisis, where no paradigm is clearly "in control." A paradigm shift occurs when a new paradigm replaces a previous one; a transition that Kuhn calls a *scientific revolution*. Kuhn characterizes the nature of a scientific revolution as follows:

Like the choice between competing political institutions, that between competing paradigms proves to be a choice between incompatible modes of community life. Because it has that character, the choice is not and cannot be determined merely by the evaluative procedures characteristic of normal science, for these depend in part upon a particular paradigm, and that paradigm is at issue. When paradigms enter, as they must, into a debate about paradigm choice, their role is necessarily circular.[2]

Kuhn likens the revolutionary nature of paradigm shifts to "gestalt switches" because the scientist perceives a different world or "a new gestalt" after a paradigm shift. New facts, obscured by the previous paradigm, become readily apparent after the shift. For example, western astronomers did not notice certain changes in the heavens until the 17th century; whereas the Chinese had recorded the appearance of new stars and sunspots centuries earlier. Kuhn attributes this difference to the fact that the western paradigm assumed that the heavens were immutable, while the Chinese one did not. Similarly, Aristotle measured a pendulum's weight, height, and the time it took to achieve rest, while Galileo, aware of Archimedes work on floating bodies and the impetus theory, measured different factors.

Since the proponents of competing paradigms see a different world, they cannot adequately communicate and do not share a common body of observational data. In short, distinct paradigms lead to divergent interpretations of "the facts." Kuhn argues persuasively that the appeal to logic and/or evidence alone is insufficient to adjudicate between paradigms and, on the contrary, that aesthetic taste or other subjective criteria determine a paradigm's acceptability.

The [person] who embraces a new paradigm at an early stage must . . . have faith that the new paradigm will succeed with the many large problems that confront it, knowing only that the older paradigm has failed with a few. A decision of that kind can only be made on faith.[3]

Incommensurability

Dispute has arisen regarding a number of issues that Kuhn raises. Do paradigms dominate normal science? Do scientific observations depend upon paradigms? Are scientific revolutions paradigm shifts? But for our purposes, the most important question is "what is the relationship between successive paradigms?"

Because paradigm shifts are radical and revolutionary and since subjectivity plays a large part in the choice between them, successive paradigms are incommensurable. This is Kuhn's most provocative theme. On this point his critics have been most vehement, accusing him of advocating "mob rule" in the sciences and also of characterizing science as relativistic, subjective, and irrational. However, Kuhn disputes all of these charges.

In his more recent writings, he denies the "strong" interpretation of incommensurability, where paradigm comparisons involve category mistakes and there is no possibility of adjudicating between competing paradigms. In other words, Kuhn disavows the charge that rival paradigms cannot be evaluated or that the choice between them is arbitrary. Yet, he explicitly states that there is no objective meta-level perspective and no theory-neutral data base from which paradigms can be assessed.[4] But if this is the case, how do we know that one theory is "better" than another? How can we avoid the charge that scientific theories are historically relative? With these problems in mind, Kuhn is forced to conclude: "We may . . . have to relinquish the notion . . . that changes of paradigm carry scientists . . . closer and closer to the truth."[5]

Psychogenesis and the History of Science

Piaget's evolutionary epistemology differs from any other because it uses psychogenesis— as a kind of mental embryogenesis— to explain the history of science. As a result, he looked to established sciences—like embryology and evolutionary biology—to provide models that illuminate the evolution of knowledge. His final views about the history of science, its parallels with psychogenesis, and the mechanisms which govern the transition between stages of knowledge are found in his posthumously published work *Psychogenesis and the History of Science*.[6]

This relatively unknown work asks: Is there a relationship between cognitive development in the individual (psychogenesis) and successive theories in the history of science? In other words, does the ontogeny of reason parallel, clarify, or explain the phylogeny of reason? The fundamental thesis of the work is that psychogenesis illuminates the epistemological significance of the history of the sciences. The evidence to support this thesis derives from certain isomorphisms between the two domains, and the strength of these parallels is central to the issue of whether the analysis of change can (profitably) be extended from one domain to the other.

Specifically, Piaget claimed to have uncovered "common mechanisms" governing the transition between successive psychogenetic stages and successive periods in the history of science. These common mechanisms justify the view that scientific change is progressive. It is important to note, however, that the two domains are not perfectly symmetrical, and he does not claim that ontogeny literally recapitulates phylogeny. Instead, it is the mechanisms mediating the transition from one developmental stage to the next in individual cognitive development which are isomorphic with those mediating transitions from one scientific theory to its successors.

The Convergence of Two Fields

Piaget argued that a parallelism exists between the way concepts—such as time or space—and cognitive operations—such as addition or subtraction—are formed at elementary levels of psychic development and their evolution at more abstract levels. Furthermore, the epistemological significance of concepts and operations is not independent of their construction, thus, the epistemological significance of conceptual tools does not admit merely of a synchronic analysis.

In vivid contrast to philosophers of science like Kuhn, Piaget maintained from the outset that the construction of knowledge is sequential, so that stages in the development of knowledge result from previous possibilities and, at the same time, open up future possibilities. These constructions are due to the reflective abstractions which move intellectual evolution along.

Reflective abstractions reorganize the concepts and operations acquired at lower levels of cognitive development and project them onto higher levels. For example, by generalizing the operation of subtraction, by abstracting the operation and then projecting it into another domain, the negative numbers are constructed. A further generalization and abstraction—due for instance, to one's inability to arrive at whole number solutions when computing square roots— leads to the construction of the irrational numbers. Finally, we construct the imaginary numbers by reflecting on the square roots of negative numbers. Thus, through reflection, we abstract the essence of the operation and project it into another domain. According to Piaget, the evidence derived from the study of the development of ideas in both children and the history of science suggests that both psychogenesis and the history of science exemplify the process of reflective abstraction.

But does this developmental approach really elucidate the epistemological significance of the history of science? While it is generally accepted that scientific theories cannot be dissociated from their historical context and that the history or genesis of a scientific concept is relevant to its epistemic significance, it is not normally thought that their epistemic significance depends exclusively upon a diachronic analysis. But Piaget believed that the stages in the evolution of cognitive concepts and scientific theories illuminate the epistemic significance of such concepts and theories because both processes— psychogenesis and the history of science—reorganize what is inherited from the preceding stage. Furthermore, both processes are governed by common mechanisms and share common problems. If this can be demonstrated, the relationship between the two kinds of research is secure.

In order to strengthen the connection between psychogenesis and the history of science, Piaget delineated three problems that they both share: 1) the problem of determining the relative contributions of experience and the subject's operational structures in the elaboration of knowledge; 2) the problem of the relationship between the subject and the objects of knowledge; and 3) the question of whether knowledge is pre-formed or constructed. He claimed that all of the analogies between the historical construction of scientific knowledge and psychogenetic development show that knowledge is a constructive process. In both domains the subject is active in a process where structures build upon preceding structures.

Nevertheless, a problem arises. If the state of knowledge depends upon past constructions, then knowledge is relative to those constructions. Does this lead to the conclusion that what we call knowledge results from an arbitrary diversity of past constructions? Piaget answered that, though constructions sometimes proceed along different paths, these paths may be coordinated at a later date when new cognitive tools evolve. He offered wave-particle duality as an example of apparently conflicting results which one day may be coordinated. This suggests that diversity of paths does not necessarily imply relativism.

Moreover, Piaget expressed optimism about future coordinations because of the underlying premise that mind and reality interact. This interaction takes place at two junctions: 1) the terminal junction of experiencing the world through our senses; and 2) the initial junction where the mind is joined to the body and the body to the physical world. Thus, no matter how far mental constructions travel from empirical phenomena, they are still connected to those phenomena. Even though different constructions may converge when new cognitive tools develop, these coordinations or convergencies are not predetermined for two reasons: 1) because the coordinations cannot be achieved until the constructions are in place; and 2) because nature itself is always evolving.

The present state of cognitive structures in biological organisms is determined by both the environment and their ontogenetic and phylogenetic history. Knowledge is never a state, it is a process which can be understood only by historico-critical analysis. Most importantly, there are no universal structures in cognitive development, since structures continually evolve; rather, the universal processes, whether one considers psychogenesis or the history of science, are functional processes. These functional invariants operate at all levels of biological and cognitive development, providing stability during the transformation of cognitive structures.

What are these universal functions which unite the fields of cognitive development and philosophy of science? They are the assimilation of new elements into preceding structures, and the accommodation of those structures to fit the acquisitions. These functional processes result in a balance or equilibrium between organisms and their environment, and they adapt the organism to the environment. As we recall, the entire process is referred to as equilibration or autoregulation—essentially, the adaptation of organisms to their environment. In the biological domain, equilibration involves the assimilation of, for example, air, food, or water from the environment and the subsequent biological accommodation to what has been assimilated. The result re-establishes the organism's biological equilibrium. In the epistemological domain, equilibration involves assimilation of, for example, concepts, ideas, or beliefs, and the subsequent epistemological accommodation to these assimilations. The result re-establishes epistemological equilibrium. If this is correct, then scientific knowledge is an extension of universal biological functioning, and the growth of scientific knowledge is governed by the same mechanisms that govern biological and psychological evolution.

General Mechanisms

What are the general mechanisms that govern the construction of knowledge? Piaget mentioned several types of mechanisms, but the most important ones relate to reasoning. Reason involves empirical abstractions—classifying physical objects into classes—and reflective abstractions which, we may recall, project onto a higher level what is derived from concepts and operations. In addition, the general cognitive processes or functional invariants—assimilation and accommodation leading to equilibrium—are indispensable for the construction of new knowledge. (These may also be thought of as mechanisms.) Most importantly, a new transitional mechanism governing the construction of knowledge was introduced:

> It is a mechanism that leads from intra-object (object analysis) to inter-object (analyzing relations or transformations) to trans-object (building of structures) levels of analysis . . . the generality of this triplet . . . undoubtedly constitutes the best of the arguments in favor of a constructivist epistemology.[7]

This intra-inter-trans sequence corresponds to constants in psychogenetic development that had been confirmed by years of painstaking empirical study—centration on elements, on their transformation, and finally on their place in the total structure. In the history of science, this sequence manifests itself as: 1) knowledge of the interrelationships of states; 2) understanding them as the result of transformations; and 3) discovering transformations as manifestations and variations of total structures.

Much of *Psychogenesis and the History of Science*[8] traced the intra-inter-trans sequence in the history of the sciences. Euclidean geometry, for example, was concerned with the internal relationship between figures and may be termed *intrafigural*. Later periods, characterized by the emergence of analytical and projective geometry, concerned themselves with "the transformations relating the figures according to various forms of correspondence" and may be called *interfigural*. Finally, the *transfigural* period was characterized by the predominance of structures, as in Klein's Erlangen Program.

The evolution of algebra exhibits similar stages. The *intraoperational* stage involved the solutions to specific equations or the relationship between internal elements. The discovery in the eighteenth century that equations could be transformed and solutions discovered that were otherwise unattainable characterizes the *interoperational* stage. These transformations were then systematized with the discovery of groups and other algebraic structures in the *transoperational* stage.

The work also traced this sequence in the history of mechanics. Newtonian mechanics represents an *intrafactual* stage, the mechanics of Lagrange and Hamilton an *interfactual* stage, and algebraic microphysics a *transfactual* stage. Throughout the history of science, this general mechanism, the intra-inter-trans sequence, is at work in the development of science.

Drawing from his studies of cognitive development, Piaget noted parallels between stages in the history of science and the corresponding stages of cognitive development. For instance, the sequence in the history of algebra corresponds to the sequence by which logico-mathematical thinking develops in children. The preoperational, concrete operational, and formal operational stages of cognitive development correspond to intraoperational, interoperational, and transoperational stages of algebraic development.

When we deal with primitive scientific thought, the parallels between the stages of psychogenesis and the history of science are striking. For example, the history of the notion of impetus can be divided into four main periods. The first period was characterized by the two Aristotelian driving forces, the next by the recourse to a single driving force, then the discovery of the impetus, and finally the concept of acceleration. These periods correspond to the way the concept of impetus develops through the four stages of psychological development (sensorimotor, preoperational, concrete operational and formal operational). In other words, Aristotle thought about physics like a child. The book provides a number of examples of isomorphic development of concepts in psychogenesis and the history of science. In fact, the isomorphisms are so striking that anyone committed to the idea of progressive cognitive development in individuals would accept the same in the history of science. Piaget concluded that the overwhelming evidence suggests that the mechanisms governing the transition from one psychological state to the next are isomorphic with those governing the development of theories and ideas in the history of science.

While the stages of development in early scientific theories and psychogenesis are isomorphic, contemporary scientific theories occur at such high levels of abstraction that the striking parallels between them and psychogenesis break down. When we deal with contemporary scientific theories, the commonality between their development and psychogenesis occurs in terms of the mechanisms which characterize the transition between successive stages. As we have seen, the most important of these mechanisms leads from the intra to inter to trans levels of analysis.

Epistemic Frameworks and Scientific Change

So far we have focused upon the internal functions which regulate the interaction between the objects of knowledge and the subject's cognitive instruments. But isn't the process of assimilating from the environment conditioned by a "social system of meanings?" One needs to explain the extent to which assimilation is conditioned by and dependent upon some social system of meanings. The emphasis on the social environment affirms the view that social transmission and environmental influence play a significant role in epistemic development. The history of science provides clear examples of the way frameworks of meaning are inserted between subjects and objects and the extent to which such frameworks condition our interpretation of the objective referents of knowledge. For example, during the scientific revolution of the seventeenth century there occurred an alteration in the system of meaning, or what Piaget called a shift in the epistemological framework. Such shifts—which reformulate the problems constitutive of scientific inquiry—are themselves the product of both exogenous and endogenous factors.

The exogenous factor of the epistemic framework is the social paradigm. Long before Kuhn wrote on the subject, Piaget recognized that scientific theories change through time and that social paradigms largely determine the course of scientific research. While research usually takes place within a scientific framework, research may facilitate a change in framework when the concentration of effort to resolve certain problems results in new questions or perspectives. The concentration of effort on certain problems and not others often depends upon social groups demanding solutions to them. Consider that a good portion of the development of classical mechanics responded to the demand to improve artillery. Different problems would have led scientific inquiry down another path. Scientific knowledge depends then, to a large extent, upon the requirements of the given society. In this sense, the social paradigm conditions the course of scientific development. Likewise, the decision to pursue nuclear rather than solar energy exemplifies the influence of social groups—not epistemic perspectives—on the direction of scientific research.

The endogenous factor of the epistemic framework is the epistemic *paradigm*. Deciding which theories, ideas, and concepts belong to the conceptual apparatus that the scientific community shares is based upon endogenous factors. For instance, Newton's mechanics was not accepted in his own day as scientific by the Cartesians or Leibnizians because it did not satisfy their requirements for being scientific. In other words, since it did not provide physical explanations of phenomena, it did not fit into the current epistemic paradigm. When Newton's explanations became universally accepted, they constituted their own epistemic paradigm. This particular paradigm restricted the notion of science to the mechanistic and reductionistic, a restriction which determined scientific thinking until the 1920s.

The epistemological framework of a society results from the interplay of the exogenous social paradigm and the endogenous epistemic paradigm. This interaction of exogenous and endogenous forces typifies the role of the functional invariants in scientific transformations. Epistemic frameworks condition the way society thinks about problems, solutions, and the type of science that develops in a society. For example, the Aristotelian conception of the world as static impeded the formulation of the law of inertia since, according to Aristotle, static objects need some force to move them or they will return to their natural state of rest. This epistemic framework renders the concept of inertia inconceivable. The Chinese, whose conception of the world was one of radical flux, had no problem conceiving of a law of inertia five centuries before Christ. Different conceptions of the world—distinct epistemic frameworks—lead to distinct scientific explanations. In addition, epistemic frameworks function as ideologies.

> Once a given epistemic framework is constituted, it becomes impossible to dissociate the contribution of the social component from the one that is intrinsic to the cognitive system. That is, once

it is constituted, the epistemic framework begins to act as an ideology which conditions the further development of science.[9]

The framework serves as an obstacle to scientific development outside of its boundaries, and only in moments of crisis does the shift take place from one epistemic framework to another. Scientific progress and the search for new explanations result from changes in the epistemic framework. Understanding scientific progress in this way relates closely to the contemporary dispute regarding the development of science. In order to situate his position, Piaget compared it with other contemporary views.

It is well-known that Thomas Kuhn argues that science is characterized by revolutionary paradigm shifts. The salient epistemological implication for Kuhn, as we have seen, concerns incommensurability and the lack of progress in science. P. K. Feyerabend takes Kuhn's position even further, arguing that scientific theories are discontinuous, irrational, and fully incommensurable. Feyerabend differs from Kuhn by rejecting the concept of normal science and defending "pluralism," the position that at any given time a number of competing paradigms coexist. Paradigms may be contradictory or inconsistent, but scientists choose whichever one satisfies their present needs.[10] An entirely different account has been presented by Karl Popper, who claims that there exists a well-defined criterion by which we can choose between theories, i.e., falsification. In his view, science progresses by discarding falsified theories.[11] Another position has been advanced by Imre Lakatos, who argues that science progresses in terms of the dynamics of the "sequences of interrelated theories." These sequences he calls "research programs," and the shift between research programs is accomplished by a form of refutation which he calls "sophisticated falsificationism." This view denies that a "crucial experiment" overthrows a scientific theory, while still advocating a rationality to scientific change. Lakatos' program essentially elaborates what is entailed in sophisticated falsificationism.

While Kuhn and Feyerabend maintain that science is basically irrational, they try, nonetheless, to describe the way science actually proceeds. On the other hand, Popper and Lakatos argue for the rationality of science and attempt to establish the norms and rules by which science progresses. However, all of these philosophers—as well as Stephen Toulmin and N. Russell Hanson—have something in common with Piaget. They all appeal to the history of science to support their assertions, disputing the positivist's analysis that scientific knowledge is concerned with a rational reconstruction of scientific knowledge independent of the process of discovery. But the way these philosophers of science interpret the process of discovery differs profoundly, and no consensus has been reached regarding the nature of scientific change.

While all of these philosophers concern themselves with whether or not the replacement of one theory by another is rationally justified, they all neglect the question of how the transition between theories actually occurs. Piaget thought this question paramount and answered it by invoking the close connection between psychogenesis and the history of science. The transition between successive theories he described as follows: One theory surpasses another, and the theory that is surpassed becomes integrated into the theory that surpasses it. Still, the continuity that results from the regulatory mechanisms and functional invariants operative in cognitive development does not exclude discontinuities. In fact, as we have seen, the regulatory mechanisms and functional invariants ensure that discontinuities will result in the process. These discontinuities, discoveries, or leaps in the history of science result from reflective abstractions. Concepts and operations thus display their own internal stability, resist perturbations, and can simultaneously be re-equilibrated to a higher structure.

To put it differently, Piaget viewed scientific progress as a process of successive constructions. He was most concerned with the epistemological problem of accounting for the change between successive theories, and the evidence, he argued, reveals that these changes are governed by similar mechanisms whether one considers the transitions between stages in psychogenesis or in the development of algebra, geometry, and mechanics. Contrary to the various philosophers of science we have mentioned, Piaget believed in the importance of empirical research—both psychological and historical—in determining the way cognitive development actually proceeds.[12] The fact that common mechanisms govern the transition between successive stages of both psychogenesis and the history of science explains both the continuity and progressive character of their developments. In addition, this fact elucidates other issues in the philosophy of science as well.

Progress in Science

Having seen that the question of how epistemic frameworks change parallels the contemporary debate concerning the growth of scientific knowledge, we might consider what Piaget's theory contributes to this debate regarding two basic issues: 1) the commensurability or incommensurability of scientific theories; and 2) the question of whether or not one can speak of scientific progress. These issues provide a vivid contrast between Piaget and theorists like Kuhn and Feyerabend.

Piaget clearly rejected the incommensurability of scientific theories because old theories are usually integrated into new ones as follows. Theories are composed of observables and theoretical constructions. The observables correspond to the properties of reality that can be measured or observed; the theoretical constructions involve coordinations and interrelations among observables. The decisive step in the transition between theories occurs when the theoretical constructions of one theory become observables in another. For example, space and time, theoretical constructions in classical mechanics, become observables in relativity theory because they acquire measurable properties. It may be objected that this does not happen in all cases, but at least sometimes the old theory is preserved as a special case of the new theory. When this happens, there is a discontinuity between what is observable, but a developmental continuity in terms of the lower theory's integration into the higher one.

It is by the process of reflective abstraction that the elements of the lower theory are projected, restructured, and reorganized onto the higher theory. The form of the old theory is abstracted—the continuity of theories—and restructured—the discontinuity of theories. The process by which one theory takes the place of another and the increased equilibrium or increasing equilibrium that results provides an answer to the issue of incommensurability. Theories can be compared in terms of their ability to solve our problems—those that solve them result in greater equilibrium.

Turning to the second issue, do successive scientific theories merely change, or are some theories "better" than others? On this issue Piaget's position is clear: he believed in epistemic progress. His views on the subject of scientific progress were clearly articulated in his multi-volume *Introduction à l'épistémologie génétique*, where he gave at least two reasons for believing in epistemic progress. First, he maintained that reason must evolve rationally, since to assume that reason evolves randomly and irrationally is self-contradictory. Because Piaget believed reason evolves rationally—that later epistemic structures are better than prior ones—he was committed to epistemic progress. Unfortunately, this reply clearly begs the question.

The second reason he accepted progress in the history of science derived from the problem of "reference points." If we presuppose a reference point—for instance, that adults understand more adequately than children—then we can easily determine whether a child makes epistemic progress. We need only gauge the compatibility of the child's knowledge with an adult's. The greater the child's compatibility with adult knowledge, the greater the epistemic progress. However, we cannot assume that contemporary scientific knowledge is better than previous scientific knowledge because we would again beg the question. How can this problem be resolved? How could one claim that scientific knowledge progresses without a reference point from which to make such an assessment?

Piaget resolved this issue by generalizing the results from his investigations of psychogenesis. Since he was convinced that the ontogenesis of knowledge is progressive, and since such striking parallels exist between psychogenesis and the evolution of ideas in the history of science, one may infer, he argued, that the history of science exhibits epistemic progress. Nevertheless, he was careful to distinguish this view from one which presupposes directionality or teleology in evolution, since the progress of cognitive evolution must be discovered after the fact by a posteriori analysis. Since the evidence shows that psychogenesis manifests epistemic progress, he inferred that all intellectual evolution tends toward greater organization and equilibrium. Remember also that he was informed by the idea that ontogeny recapitulates phylogeny and by the idea that all organisms seek biological and epistemological equilibrium. In fact, the notion of equilibrium shows why some theories are better than others; some are more equilibrated than others. In essence this means that they provide for a better balance between epistemic subjects and the objects of their knowledge. Thus, the concept of equilibration explains epistemic change, scientific progress, and scientific rationality.

The process by which knowledge grows may be neatly summarized. Assimilation from the cognitive environment alters the internal environment often resulting in a kind of cognitive disequilibrium. This disequilibrium stimulates creative thinking—i.e., reflective abstractions—and the process results in the adoption of new theories/ beliefs/concepts, etc. as part of an epistemic framework. This reveals how the exogenous environment interacts with endogenous cognitive structures in the formation of new knowledge, and it demonstrates how the evolution of knowledge depends upon the subject's constructions, which are at one and the same time creative and interpretive of reality. Finally, it illustrates how science is, contrary to Kuhn and others, a process of evolution toward something—an increasing balance, fit, or equilibrium between mind and reality.

Conclusion: Constructive Evolution

Piaget summarized his findings in *Psychogenesis and the History of Science* by classifying the most general aspects of the similarities between psychogenesis and the history of science. There are *instruments*—the senses—that are common to the acquisition of all knowledge. These instruments are involved in the assimilation of objects and events, and the corresponding accommodation of the subject's existing structures. These instruments then initiate various *processes*, such as the search for reasons to justify abstractions and generalizations. Finally, there are the two general *mechanisms* in both psychogenesis and the history of science: 1) the intra-inter-trans sequence; and 2) the general mechanism of equilibration.

If Piaget is right—that knowledge is acquired by instruments which initiate processes and which are in turn governed by general mechanisms—then the fields of cognitive psychology and philosophy of science may be unified. It is not surprising that there are similarities between these fields since the central problem for cognitive psychology, philosophy of science, and epistemology is the same: how does knowledge develop? On the final page of *Psychogenesis and the History of Science*, Piaget reminded the reader that the goal of genetic epistemology was to show how cognitive structures have their basis in biological organization. According to Piaget, the isomorphisms between psychogenesis and the history of science provide further evidence for this thesis. He concluded the essay by comparing cognitive structures with Ilya Prigogine's "dissipative structures." Not only are the most cognitive sophisticated structures ultimately linked to principles of biological organization, but they are linked also "to certain forms of dynamic equilibrium in physics."[13]

Piaget claimed that cognitive equilibrations are analogous to dissipative structures in at least five ways: 1) they concern dynamic equilibria regarding exchanges with the environment; 2) these exchanges stabilize the structures through regulations; 3) equilibration is characterized as a form of "self-organization"; 4) the structures can only be understood in terms of their past history; and 5) the stability of structures is a function of their complexity. This comparison demonstrated that his conception of equilibrium extended downward from cognitive structures to organic nature and ultimately to equilibria in physics. However, he admitted that the structures differ in an important respect. Cognitive structures are integrated into the structures that surpass them. Understood in this way, one could say that the growth of scientific knowledge is the ultimate manifestation of self-organizing systems, and the most definitive manifestation of a self-organizing universe.

Piaget's investigations had confirmed his belief that all levels of cognitive development seek to adapt the mind to reality, thereby extending the organism's basic biological functioning. In fact, this is the main conclusion of Piaget's lifelong work—that the growth of knowledge, whether psychogenetic or scientific, is governed by common mechanisms and can be described as a process of constructive evolution.[14]

CHAPTER 6

Assessing Piaget's Conception of Evolution

Piaget's earliest thoughts regarding evolution previewed his most mature ones. For instance, the concepts of organization, equilibrium, and interactionism already appeared in the autobiographical novel *Recherche*. There he held that the reciprocal preservation of parts and whole in any organized totality is an unstable equilibrium, due to the interference from other systems and disruption by environmental factors. Furthermore, he argued that the organism responds to this disruption with internal modifications designed to ensure its preservation and organization, prefiguring Piaget's mature views concerning structuralism and equilibrium. In addition, the emphasis on exogenous environmental factors as the initiators of endogenous restructuring was also present. Yet his core ideas were nebulous at this point. The nature of structures, particularly psychological ones, and the specific role equilibrium played in their development was yet to be investigated. Finally, the precise way in which the interaction of environmental factors and organized totalities brought about endogenous restructuring remained unresolved.

The Development of Piaget's Theory

The Early Account

It was his studies of cognitive development in children that provided Piaget with the opportunity to formulate his first conception of the evolutionary/developmental process. Essentially, he argued that the subject's intellectual structures adapt to the objects of its knowledge. By observing the development of language, thought, judgment, and reasoning in the child, he determined that logical thinking develops by reflecting upon one's actions. He conceived a process whereby the external world is internalized in terms of formal categories that describe it, foreshadowing his later concept of cognitive phenocopy. He also realized that logical thinking was a form of psychological equilibrium, but he did not yet know how cognitive reflection moved intellectual evolution to progressively higher levels. He further observed that mind developed in an orderly fashion and that higher levels of thinking are characterized by equilibrium. But he needed to further specify the laws governing this process and the manner in which the mind/reality interaction's initiates intellectual growth.

Initially, Piaget hesitated to extend whatever conclusions he might reach regarding psychological development to epistemology. While psychological laws could be extended to epistemology, he claimed, "We are in no way suggesting . . . that our psychological results will admit straight away of being generalized into epistemological laws."[1] While he was convinced from the beginning that such an extension was possible, his affirmation of the hypothesis was withheld until the history of science had been investigated. Forty years later he was less tentative in his claim: "The fundamental hypothesis of genetic epistemology is that there is a parallelism between the progress made in the logical and rational organization of knowledge and the corresponding formative psychological processes."[2]

The early psychological studies had reinforced his belief that psychological development arises from the interaction of the organism and environment and that this process leads to greater stability or equilibrium between the two. In addition, he believed that an analysis of psychogenetic development would shed light on epistemological issues, particularly those concerning the growth of scientific knowledge. In addition to the evidence afforded by psychogenetic investigation, his biological research was also relevant. His biological investigations revealed that restructuring was induced by the organism's activity instead of by a passive reception of the environment.

The Origins of Intelligence

Piaget presented his first detailed account of evolution in *The Origins of Intelligence in Children*. There he introduced the concept of functional invariants, the constant elements amidst the process of structural change. The basic biological activity of the organism is governed by these invariant functions, and intellectual function is the extension of biological functioning. Thus, he concluded that intellectual functioning must be governed by the same principles as biological functioning. These conclusions were based upon the detailed studies of children which revealed that a version of interactionism accounted for psychogenetic development. The detailed nature of this interaction would be expressed much later in the theory of the phenocopy, but the seeds of Piaget's rejection of both Lamarckism and Darwinism were taking shape. The psychological equivalent of either theory could not account for the developing intellect; only organism/environment interactionism could do so.

Next, Piaget determined that the history of science provided adequate evidence to extend the evolutionary model from the individual knower to the history of science. He found that the history of science, like psychogenesis, could best be explained by subject/object interactionism. He also found that the history of science, particularly mathematics, displayed the crucial role played by reflective abstraction in the evolution of scientific knowledge. Reflective abstraction accounted for both the continuity and the novelty of scientific thinking, just as it had done in psychogenesis.

Most importantly, these studies convinced Piaget that knowledge evolves in a progressive direction. Both the history of science and the development of the individual's intellectual structures reveal a directionality. His final position specified how the organism's activity directs evolution.

The Final Position

The beginning of a synthesis of Piaget's thinking was evident in *Biology and Knowledge*. There the essence of the relationship between organic regulations and cognitive processes was presented in detail. He affirmed the continuity between organic and cognitive evolution in terms of *autoregulation*, the universal characteristic of all life which drives evolution from the simplest organic forms to the most complex forms of scientific and mathematical thought. Autoregulation is synonymous with equilibration, the evolutionary process which applies to both organic and cognitive reality.

All of Piaget's previous theorizing on the topic of evolution culminated in *Behavior and Evolution*. There he claimed that the organism's behavior is a means of self-regulation and that disequilibrium between behavior and the environment can be transferred to the genome. The emphasis on behavior and phenocopy were the new and distinctive elements of Piaget's final model of evolution. Though the emphasis on behavior was novel to the theory, he had implicitly maintained that the subject's activity was important in evolution from the beginning, regardless of whether he considered the evolution of snail's shells, children's thinking, or the history of science. Internalizing the external world, making it part of one's own structure, results from the organism's activity and brings organism/mind and environment/reality into contact. It is the interplay between the subject's activity, the genetic variations generated in response to that activity, and the phenocopy mediating between behavior and the genotype which epitomizes constructive evolution. In essence, Piaget argued that the organizational tendencies manifest in evolution result from the behavior of the organism. This mature model of evolution reiterated his rejection—evident from the very beginning—of both the Lamarckian and Darwinian models.

Admittedly, it is easy to be puzzled when considering how his conception of evolution applies at various levels of reality. Are not development and evolution different things altogether? Perhaps this confusion results from the fact that he made no distinction between biological and cognitive evolution/development. This point has been put succinctly by Brian Rotman.

> The very distinction [between evolution and development] is artificial in Piaget's system, since within it knowledge, psychological structure, and physiological structure are all of a piece, so that the conventional meaning of evolution—as it occurs in the evolution of biological forms—merges with Piaget's use of it for knowledge.[3]

We might conclude our discussion of the development of Piaget's theory by summarizing his basic conception of the evolutionary process. In simplest form, cognitive evolution is the adaptation of the subject's intellectual structures to reality, while biological evolution is the adaptation of organism's biological structure to the environment. In the cognitive case, adaptation consists in the assimilation of new perceptions, ideas, and events into existing schemata and the subsequent accommodation of those schemata to the materials assimilated. The process aims at achieving cognitive equilibrium. Analogously, biological adaptation consists in the assimilation of elements of the environment and the subsequent accommodation of the organism explained in terms of the theory of phenocopy. In both the cognitive and biological cases, adaptation is a two-fold process of assimilation and accommodation which aims at equilibrium.

In essence, the connection between the biological and the cognitive is in terms of the adaptational or organizational principles that apply at all levels of biological functioning. These principles apply to cognitive functioning as well, since cognition extends biological functioning. In other words, since thought is an activity of the organism it must be governed by the same laws of organization as the organism itself. In short, these "laws of organization" are universal—applicable to all living systems—and reality is subordinated to these evolutionary laws. While cognitive and biological structures differ, due primarily to the fact that successive structures "overtake" previous ones by generating novelty, both result from the organism's basic functioning. This continual process of organization and adaptation moving toward more equilibrated states guarantees evolutionary progress and is the essence of Piaget's conception of evolution. Through painstaking empirical analysis, he had uncovered the laws that govern the process of change.

Problems with the Theory

The Gap between Biology and Knowledge

One might object that evolutionary theory should not be extended from biology to epistemology. Evolutionary theory applies, so the critic argues, to organic reality only and cannot be utilized to explain epistemology. If this is so, then talk of intellectual evolution or any reciprocal impact of epistemological studies on evolutionary theory is empty. And in fact some contemporary philosophers have opposed all evolutionary epistemologies.[4] But what exactly is it they oppose? What is evolutionary epistemology?

The modern evolutionary view of the human mind began with Darwin and was championed in the nineteenth century by Herbert Spencer. Evolutionary epistemology analyzes the philosophical repercussions of Darwin's scientific discovery of which the most important is that cognitive activities are products of evolution. The contemporary evolutionary epistemologist Donald T. Campbell states that "an evolutionary epistemology would be at minimum an epistemology taking cognizance of and compatible with man's status as a product of biological and social evolution."[5] The proponents of the view that cognitive faculties are evolutionary products includes the eminent scientists Julian Huxley, George G. Simpson, Jacques Monod, C. H. Waddington, Konrad Lorenz, and E. O. Wilson, virtually all other contemporary biologists, and of course Jean Piaget. In addition, the list of philosophers who may be called evolutionary epistemologists, or who have at least proposed an evolutionary interpretation of the Kantian categories, include William James, C.S. Pierce, Ernst Cassirer, Karl Popper, Stephen Toulmin, Hans Reichenbach, R.W. Sellers, Emile Meyerson, and W.V. Quine.

The near unanimity of agreement concerning the basic claims of evolutionary epistemology does not guarantee their truth, but does suggest that evolutionary epistemology is, at the very least, plausible. Inasmuch as evolution has been established beyond a reasonable doubt as a historical fact—given the overwhelming evidence provided by fossil, biochemical, anatomical, embryological, and other sciences—it is certain that cognitive faculties must have arisen in the evolutionary process. Thus, a complete account of human cognition must include an evolutionary component. Nevertheless, extending evolutionary theory from body to mind is not a move in formal logic and the extension must be evaluated in terms of the factual or empirical similarities that exist between the two realms.

But is it enough to claim that there are analogies between biology and knowledge? Do analogies alone justify an evolutionary explanation of knowledge? Piaget did not think so. Analogies are necessary but not sufficient conditions for arguing that a theory of evolution is applicable to both life and mind. What is needed is to demonstrate that cognition is essentially biological.

In *Biology and Knowledge* Piaget argued that the structural isomorphisms and functional connections between biology and cognition demonstrate that cognition is essentially biological. In the first place, cognition is biological to the extent that it depends on the hereditary transmission of physical structures like the nervous system. Second, automatic behavioral reactions like reflexes depend upon inherited physical structures. While these reflexes play only a minor role in human intelligence, they do influence the newborn in its initial encounter with the world. From this encounter develop the psychological structures that form the basis for intellectual activity.

Intelligence is biological since it depends upon the hereditary transmission of physical structures—which place limits on intellectual functioning—and the behavioral reactions which are influential in the first few days of life. But the most important biological factors that influence cognition are the invariant functions of organization and adaptation. Organization—the tendency of all species to systematize or organize their processes into coherent systems—is common to both physiology and psychology. It is the universal tendency of all forms of life to organize their structures into higher-order structures. Adaptation—the tendency of organisms to adapt to the environment—is the other universal and invariant biological function that manifests itself at the cognitive level. These invariant functions apply to all living systems independent of their organizational properties. According to Piaget, thought is an activity of the organism and therefore subject to the same laws of organization and adaptation as the organism itself. Cognition is essentially biological because it evolved from biological structures and functions according to the same invariants.

Nevertheless, the reduction of cognitive functioning back to the biological is at best only partial. That is because structures do not evolve randomly into new structures but evolve according to the operation of the invariant functions. Without the invariant functions there would be no evolution—merely random change—and structures could be reduced to prior structures. But Piaget claimed that the functional invariants operating on lower structures produce higher and genuinely novel structures. These structures cannot be reduced to physiology because they possess their own intrinsic properties and they overtake or reconstruct previous forms. Piaget's studies in both psychogenesis and the history of science provided the evidence for this claim. Thus, since knowledge is essentially biological, we are justified in advancing an evolutionary explanation of human knowledge.

Ontogeny and Phylogeny

As we have seen, Piaget did not have direct access to the evolution of cognitive faculties in the history of the species, so he studied children as member instances of the cognitive evolution of the species as a whole. Just as biology uses embryology as a model for morphological development in the species, psychogenesis in children provides a model for the evolution of cognitive functioning in the species. In this way he believed epistemology could be empirical. But is this approach justified? Is the connection between ontogeny and phylogeny close enough for Piaget's purposes? If it is not, then a conception of evolution applicable to psychogenesis is irrelevant to the development of the cognitive faculties in the species or to any conception of organic evolution. If the relationship between ontogeny and phylogeny is strong, then the case for an evolutionary phylogenesis of reason is unmistakable, since the ontogenesis of reason had been established empirically.

A classic formulation of the relationship between ontogeny and phylogeny was suggested by Karl Ernst von Baer and modified by Ernst Haeckel. It is the bio-genetic law which states that "ontogeny is a recapitulation of phylogeny."[6] Recently, the history and central issues of this relationship have been explored by Stephen J. Gould in his book *Ontogeny and Phylogeny*. While Gould criticizes the classic formulations of this relationship, noting that contemporary genetics has caused the theory to be abandoned, he is sympathetic to the basic approach. "I refuse to believe that so many of the most brilliant scientists in the history of biology consistently placed at center stage a topic of merely peripheral importance."[7] Gould testifies that many of his colleagues secretly believe such parallels enlightening and he concurs: "Evolutionary changes must be expressed in ontogeny, and phyletic information must therefore reside in the development of individuals."[8] So it seems that contemporary biology has a place for a general recapitulation theory. Certainly biologists deny that human embryos ever pass through fish-like or reptile-like stages and almost all of them claim that the contemporary evidence refutes a literal interpretation of Haeckel's law. But this in no way denies that such a comparison has heuristic value.

Nevertheless, conceptualizing the precise nature of the relationship between the two areas is difficult. In the case of Haeckel, the relationship is particularly problematic because he postulated a direct effect of phylogenesis on ontogenesis. While Gould denies Haeckel's claim, he suggests the plausibility of the claim that external constraints regulate both processes. According to Gould, Piaget's research with children demonstrates how external constraints operate on both phylogeny and ontogeny without Haeckelian recapitulation.[9] In other words, ontogenetic and phylogenetic development correspond because both are governed by external constraints (functional invariants). In opposition to Haeckel, ontogeny and phylogeny do not exercise any influence on each other. As we have seen, Piaget's solution to his problematic rested upon this parallelism.

> The fundamental hypothesis of genetic epistemology is that there is a parallelism between the progress made in the logical and rational organization of knowledge and the corresponding formative psychological processes. With the hypothesis, the most fruitful, most obvious field of study would be the reconstituting of human history—the history of human thinking in prehistoric man. Unfortunately, we are not very well informed in the psychology of primitive man, but there are children all around us, and it is in studying children that we have the best chance of studying the development of logical knowledge, mathematical knowledge, physical knowledge, and so forth.[10]

The move from an ontogeny of reason to a phylogeny of reason—like the one from biology to knowledge—is to be assessed on the strength of the factual and empirical similarities between the two domains. (Remembering, of course, that all knowledge is biological.) Epistemological issues are not settled a priori. The phylogeny of reason must provide the evidence to justifiably extend the model of evolution from one level to another. Just as detailed studies of psychogenetic development in children revealed striking parallels between cognitive and biological development, the development of concepts in the history of science were found to be quite similar with psychogenetic development. These two independent sequences follow similar paths because of the constraints imposed by the functional invariants—a contention supported by the strength of the factual evidence. The strength of this evidence and the validity of the claim that knowledge is biological strongly urge us to conclude that laws of process govern all evolutionary and developmental processes.

More than fifty years of research revealed that psychogenesis and the history of science are isomorphic to a significant extent. This overwhelming evidence, unavailable or unnoticed by most philosophers, gives us good reason to concur with Piaget's conclusion: both the ontogeny and phylogeny of reason are governed by invariant functions.

The Problem of Progress

Even if we grant that mind evolves and that the ontogeny of reason and phylogeny of reason are parallel, this still does not ensure that intellectual evolution is progressive. Why suppose that adult knowledge is more adequate than children's or contemporary science more adequate than earlier science? Piaget provided at least three answers to the question of progress. We will consider each in turn.

First, he maintained that the progress evident in restricted genetic epistemology can be generalized to the growth of knowledge as a whole. But Piaget must respond to the objection that he "begs the question" by simply assuming that the reference point by which progress in a given field is to be judged—in this case adult knowledge—is somehow "better" than children's knowledge. However, he never gave any definitive reason to accept this claim. Though the claim that adults know more than children is not particularly problematic, he did not establish it definitively.

Second, he assumed that reason must evolve rationally which implies progress in cognitive evolution. To assume the opposite he held to be self-contradictory. But this answer is not without difficulties. All agree that if reason evolves rationally, then cognitive faculties are reliable and there is cognitive progress. But this is precisely the point at issue—whether or not reason evolves rationally and is reliable. If it did not, then there is no reason to believe our cognitive faculties are reliable or that there is cognitive progress. Again, Piaget assumes what he is trying to prove. His argument does show that there is a connection between reason evolving rationally and cognitive reliability and progress, but it does not show that cognitive faculties evolved in this way.

His last answer invoked the process of equilibration—the idea which provided his fundamental answer to the progress issue. The demand for equilibrium directs organized totalities toward a biological, psychological, and epistemological balance between themselves and their environment. In the biological area this demand expresses itself in the physical adaptation of the organism to the environment and in the cognitive domain as the adaptation of mind to reality. The functional invariants which manifest themselves in all life processes including cognition guarantee epistemic progress.

Criticism of Biological Constructivism

Since Piaget believed that laws of form operate at all levels of reality, it is not surprising that his theory of cognitive development would have a reciprocal influence upon his biological theorizing. While his theories of psychological development have been, for the most part, well received, his theory of biological evolution has been vehemently opposed. For example, the eminent neurobiologist Jean-Pierre Changeux argued that the concept of phenocopy "corresponds to a decrease in the genetic potentialities of the organism."[11] In discussing Piaget's biological observations, Changeux claimed that *Limnaea* which adapt to different environments exhibit multiple phenotypes, whereas the so-called phenocopy displays only one. According to Changeux, "the phenocopy would not correspond to the acquisition of a new competence, but to a loss of genetic potentialities."[12] In other words, *Limnaea* in whom phenotypic adaptations become hereditarily fixed have in fact lost the genes that determine other phenotypes. Changeux, like most contemporary biologists, categorically rejected Piaget's biological theory.

> Modern theories of evolution are based on the spontaneous and random mutations of the DNA molecule and on the recombination of its segments; obviously, these views are valid in the case of higher vertebrates, and it seems difficult to imagine, at present, a molecular mechanism for Piaget's mutations "particular to the human species."[13]

And the noted molecular biologist Antoine Danchin criticized Piaget's biological theory as hopelessly out of date.

> Although it may have been possible, before the existence of molecular biology, to believe in an "instructive" or "creative" principle that would explain the determination of traits in a living organism, producing an adaptive phenocopy . . . this point is today merely an episode in the history of ideas.[14]

Danchin's explanation of phenocopy echoed Changeux's. Phenotypic adaptations occur, and in some cases become invariant, when organisms confront specialized environmental conditions. In these cases, the organism loses "the regulatory aptitudes that allowed it to change its phenotype according to the environment."[15] This loss of phenotypic variability is not detrimental in such cases because the specialized environment remains constant. Other organisms retain phenotypic variability which they exhibit when transferred back to their original environment. According to Danchin, individual phenotypes can be understood "without allowing the intervention of even the least instructive notion on the part of the environment."[16] Phenocopy does not indicate a constructive evolutionary process, "but simply a particular realization of a given program according to a strict determinism."[17] He maintained that all of the available biological evidence disputes Piaget's views.

As non-biologists we must defer to the experts who maintain that Piaget's biological theory is, at the present time, unsubstantiated. No mechanism has been identified which explains how somatic modifications, either directly or indirectly, effect the genome. There is no reason to accept Piaget's theory of biological evolution. Nevertheless, the biologists C. H. Waddington and Ludwig von Bertalanffy and the Nobel prize winning physicist/chemist Ilya Prigogine argued for theories involving feedback systems such as Piaget's. Moreover, scientific theories continually transform. Therefore an arrogant dogmatism which categorically rejects any theory other than neo-Darwinism is unwarranted.

But even if Piaget's biological theory of evolution is mistaken that does not invalidate his theory of epistemological evolution. It may be that the two kinds of evolution are not isomorphic. Of course, this would undermine much of Piaget's theorizing since he used the isomorphisms between the two to argue much of his case. In that case his epistemological theory could still turn out to be right, but for the wrong reasons!

Constructive Evolution

The Self-Organizing Universe

If evolution is characterized neither as the movement toward final causes nor as the product of chance, but as an incessant "march toward equilibrium," how does one reconcile the increasing organization of organisms with the continual disorder implied by the second law of thermodynamics? Piaget contended that organic development and the second law of thermodynamics do not contradict each other.[18] Although gradual disorder holds for closed systems, that is, ones that do not interact with the environment, organisms are open systems that assimilate order from the environment or dissipate their disorder into the environment. In this way they become increasingly ordered and complex. Piaget compared his theory of the equilibration of cognitive structures to what Prigogine called "dissipative structures." Dissipative structures dissipate their entropy into the environment.[19]

For Prigogine, the transformation from order to disorder manifests itself at the physico-chemical level.[20] Structures and their substructures continually fluctuate, and sometimes these fluctuations are powerful enough to disturb pre-existing organization. When this happens, structures either disintegrate or leap to a higher level of order. If they take the appropriate leap, they are "dissipative structures." These new structures dissipate their disorder into the environment and require more energy to sustain themselves than did the previous less-ordered structures. Throughout his works, Prigogine insists that organization arises spontaneously from disorder through a process of self-regulation.

The parallels with Piaget's theory are obvious. For Piaget, self-regulation expresses itself as the tendency toward equilibrium, and constructive evolution dispels the effects of entropy by progressive organization. From the evolution of structural forms to the understanding of quantum physics and curved space, evolution is a constructive process in which organisms become increasingly equilibrated through exchange with the environment.

This is precisely what Piaget meant when he distinguished variational from organizational evolution. While the former ensues from genetic mutation, the latter results from the organism's behavior—from its constructions. In effect, the process is not constructing us; we are constructing it!

Variational and Constructive Evolution

Contemporary geneticists insist that the genetic envelope cannot be penetrated and that it determines the range of regulations and behaviors available to the organism. By contrast, Piaget maintained that the order or structure of the milieu can pierce the so-called genetic envelope. And this exchange results in constructive evolution. The ramifications of these contrary viewpoints need to be investigated.

Molecular biology is reductionistic; the microscopic determines, and is unaffected by, the macroscopic. There exists an asymmetry of determinism between the two worlds—the causality and explanation is unidirectional. This can be seen in the claim of molecular biologists that randomness and chance cause evolution. The illustrious molecular biologist Jacques Monod provided the classic statement:

> Pure chance, absolutely free but blind at the very root of the stupendous edifice of evolution: this central concept of modern biology is no longer one among other possible or even conceivable hypotheses: it is the sole conceivable hypothesis, the only one that squares with observed and tested fact.[21]

Furthermore, Monod claimed that the indeterminacy or uncertainty operative in genetic mutations is "essential" as opposed to "operational."[22] This uncertainty does not result from our inability to determine the causes of mutations—operational uncertainty—but from purely accidental coincidences—essential uncertainty. The ultimate source of essential uncertainty is the same as for quantum events, because mutations are quantum events. The only alternative to accepting essential uncertainty, according to Monod, is to adopt fatalism.

Monod's description of evolution is paradigmatic of the received view in contemporary biology. We characterize the theses of this position to be: 1) evolution proceeds because of chance; 2) evolution is essentially irrational; 3) there is no teleology to evolution; and 4) evolution implies complete freedom, since no laws govern its process. The first thesis is definitional and follows from the overwhelming evidence of molecular biology. The second and third follow from the first, and the fourth follows from the claim that evolutionary change is "essentially" uncertain. We call this evolution variational.

Piaget's constructive evolution provides a vivid contrast. He did not deny that chance could plausibly explain the color of the butterfly, but he did not believe it sufficiently explained behavior. Can we really suppose that the specialized instincts or the adaptation of mathematics to reality arise from chance? Does chance explain the development of science or the increase in genes from bacteria to higher animals?

In addition to the few biologists who express support for something like Piaget's constructivist biology, the theory found favor with some social scientists. The psychologist and Piaget scholar Hans Furth also made a strong case for constructivism by disparaging the idea of chance. He claimed that evolutionary theories must account for evolutionary newness; how does new knowledge get into the genome? Furth maintained that postulating God or chance as the cause of new knowledge evades the question and reveals our ignorance.

Furth considered a behavior which exhibits the absurdity of a chance-based evolutionary explanation. A particular orchid imitates the shape and odor of a female wasp, and this deception attracts the male wasp for the purpose of cross-fertilization. The mind boggles at the proposal of chance mutations to explain how the orchid's genome arrives at such information because "knowledge and chance are contradictions."[23] Since chance clearly plays a role in evolution, could it be that the organism knows how to exploit chance occurrences? Furth wondered if knowledge results from the genome's assimilation of environmental perturbations and then reconciles them in some way with on-going random variations. This explanation is plausible once one assumes that the genome is alive and that the genetic envelope. though remaining intact, is not impregnable.

While recognizing the contributions of the microscopic and the effects of programming and environmental influences, Piaget denounces one-way causality and the omission of the process of equilibration/self-regulation in evolutionary transformations. It is by organizational and adaptive behaviors that the organism exploits the interaction of microscopic and macroscopic forces. It then becomes capable of transcending those forces that have hitherto constrained it. This process is not easily recognizable when biological knowledge creates new biological forms because that process is extraordinarily slow. But it is quite evident when knowledge creates new abstract forms since that process is extraordinarily rapid. In cognitive evolution the interchange between the subject's endogenous faculties and the objects of knowledge is most apparent.

We take the essential theses of constructive evolution to be: 1) evolution proceeds by organization; 2) evolution is primarily rational; 3) there is a direction to evolution; and 4) there is limited freedom in evolution because laws govern and constrain the process. The first point is definitional, the second and third follow from the first, and the fourth is a consequence of the functional invariants. We call such evolution constructive.

The key issue concerns whether evolution is fundamentally variational or organizational. Piaget's belief that the evolutionary process is organizational no doubt derived from his psychological studies. In psychological/cognitive development environmental internalization and the subsequent organization consist of the construction of cognitive schemata to represent the objects of knowledge. But did Piaget need to conclude that this internalization proceeds analogously in both biology and epistemology in order to solve his original problematic—the gap between the two?

We maintain that he did not. He needed to show only that evolution—both organic regulations and the knowledge which extends them—is a self-organizing process. The details of the specific evolutionary mechanisms then become secondary considerations. Hence, it does not matter whether the perturbations that move evolution come from the internal or external environments, only that order and organization emerge from randomness and chance. The biologist B.C. Goodwin supported this contention. He argued that the mechanisms of the neo-Darwinian model need not be abandoned if one adds a theory of self-organizing organisms. The organism as a structured whole can then be inserted between chance and selection. What is fundamental to constructive evolution is that perturbations, regardless of their origin, drive organisms to explore possibilities that enhance their organization. "These processes are characterized by the property of transforming randomness and contingency, whatever its source and nature, into appropriate order, whether cognitive or biological."[24] If this is so, then Piaget was right—evolution is constructive.

Conclusion

We conclude that evolution is a self-organizing process. Moreover, the speed of evolutionary organization increases as evolution progresses. Early in evolutionary history randomness overwhelmed the primitive organizational tendencies of matter, making progressive organization painstakingly slow. As the process progressed, as behavioral schemata became more complex, organizational tendencies increased exponentially. This expedited the process of organizational evolution. The extraordinary rate of cultural evolution, characterized by abstract cognitive representations of external reality, relegates variational evolution to virtual obscurity. Though learning itself may proceed by spontaneous reorganization of schemata—a reminder that much of our past originated in spontaneous reorganization of genetic material—its primary role is to overcome the contingencies of chance. Evolution overcomes contingency by its organizational and constructive powers which transform cognitive schemata and align them with reality.

Perhaps these considerations allow us to best situate Piaget's thought. His underlying thesis is that evolution must be directed, rational, and progressive or else it is contingent, irrational, and random. His rejection of the latter, based upon decades of studying how children learn, necessitates his acceptance of the former. Committed to a law-governed evolutionary process, Piaget is the intellectual heir of Heraclitus. The functional invariants are the laws of form which govern the process of change. Change tends toward equilibrium. It is this tendency which guarantees a progressive direction to evolution.

We conclude that though the specifics of Piaget's evolutionary theory are suspect, its general conclusion is not; biological and cognitive reality are self-organizing. This conclusion is not an article of faith, nor does it appeal to any type of vitalism, entelechy, or teleology. Rather it is inferred from a posteriori analysis of both realms of activity. All of the available evidence suggests that evolution is a process of organization; organization is a property of living things. On this basis we affirm Piaget's main thesis—*evolution is a self-organizing and constructive process.* In the final analysis, he believed that reality comes to know itself through living organisms. Nature creates consciousness and consciousness reflects upon nature. By this differentiation and subsequent interaction reality becomes self-conscious. All of Piaget's writings elaborate and reverberate this one fundamental theme: evolution is a process of thought adapting to reality.

Notes

Chapter 1

1. Jean Piaget, "Jean Piaget,"in *History of Psychology in Autobiography*, vol. 4, ed. E. G. Boring, H. S. Langeld, H. Werner, and R. M. Yerkes (Worchester, Ma.: Clark University Press, 1952), 237.

2. Ibid., 238

3. Ibid., 239

4. Ibid., 240.

5. Ibid., 241. "Sketch of a Neo-pragmatism" remains unpublished.

6. Ibid., 241-42.

7. H. E. Gruber and J. J. Voneche, eds., *The Essential Piaget* (New York: Basic Books, 1977), 48.

8. Henri Bergson, *Creative Evolution* (New York: Modern Library, 1944), xxiii-xxiv. First published 1907.

9. Ibid., xix.

10. Ibid., 194.

11. Herbert Spencer, *First Principles*, 6th ed. (Akron: Werner Co., 1900), 367. In a footnote Spencer mentions that the word "relatively" should be inserted before each antithetical clause.

12. Richard Kitchener, *Piaget's Theory of Knowledge* (New Haven: Yale University Press, 1986), 11.

13. Emile Meyerson, *Identity and Reality*, trans. K. Lowenberg (New York: Dover Publications, 1962), Chap. 1. First published 1908.

14. Jean-Claude Bringuier, *Conversations with Jean Piaget* (Chicago: University of Chicago Press, 1980), 13.

15. Jean Piaget, *Insights and Illusions of Philosophy*, trans. W. Mays. (New York: World Publishing Company, 1971), xiv.

16. Michael Chapman, *Constructive Evolution* (Cambridge: Cambridge University Press, 1988), Chapter 1.

17. For a listing of Piaget's religious writings see the bibliography in Michael Chapman, *Constructive Evolution*.

18. See Jean Piaget, *Insights and Illusions of Philosophy*. Here Piaget discussed the limited value of speculative thinking.

19. Gruber and Voneche, eds., *The Essential Piaget*, xi.

20. Chapman, *Constructive Evolution*, 437.

21. Richard Kitchener, *Piaget's Theory of Knowledge* (New Haven: Yale University Press, 1986), 6.

22. Hans Furth, *Piaget and Knowledge*, 2nd ed. (Chicago: University of Chicago Press, 1981), 285.

Chapter 2

1. Jean Piaget, "Jean Piaget," in *History of Psychology in Autobiography*, vol. 4, ed. E. G. Boring, H. S. Langeld, H. Werner, and R. M. Yerkes, (Worchester, Ma.: Clark University Press, 1952), 245.

2. These first five books which brought Piaget international acclaim were: *The Language and Thought of the Child* 1923; *Judgment and Reasoning in the Child* 1924, *The Child's Conception of the World* 1926, *The Child's Conception of Physical Causality* 1927, and *The Moral Judgment of the Child* 1932.

3. Jean Piaget, *The Language and Thought of the Child* (New York: World Publishing Co., 1973), 236-37. (Original work published 1923)

4. Jean Piaget, *Judgment and Reasoning in the Child* (Patterson, N.J.: Littlefield, Adams & Co., 1959), 170-71. (Original work published 1924)

5. Ibid., 171-72. The idea of reversibility can be understood by the following example: A child is shown two equal-length rows of eight coins each. He agrees that the rows have the same *number* of coins, but believes the number changes when one of the rows is lengthened. According to Piaget, children are not able to *reverse* the act of lengthening, i.e., they cannot maintain the belief in equivalence of number when confronting perceptual change.

6. Here we introduce the idea of stages, an important concept in Piaget's system. Stages are characterized by invariant sequences, a hierarchical relationship with successive stages, and integration or wholeness. Another important aspect of stages is the notion of "decalage." Piaget distinguishes between two types. Horizontal decalage, referring to the repetition that takes place within a single period of development and vertical decalage, referring to the repetition that occurs at different levels of functioning. For an excellent summary of the concept of stages in Piaget's work the reader is referred to John Flavell, *The Developmental Psychology of Jean Piaget*, (Princeton, N.J.: Van Nostrand Co., 1963), 19-24.

7. Jean Piaget, *The Child's Conception of Physical Causality* (New York: Harcourt, Brace and Co., 1930), 240. (Original work published 1927)

8. Ibid., 240.

9. The books which report this research are *The Origins of Intelligence in Children* 1936, *The Construction of Reality in the Child* 1937, and *Play, Dreams and Imitation in Childhood* 1945.

10. "Les races lacustres de la 'Limnaea stagnalis' L. Recherches sur les rapports de l'adaptation hereditaires avec le milieu," *Bulletin Biologique de la France et la Belgique* 63, (1929): 424-55. See also, "L'adaptation de la limnaea stagnalis aux milieux lacustres de la Suisse romande," *Revue Suisse de Zoologie* 36, (1929): 263-531.

11. Jean Piaget, "Jean Piaget," 250.

12. Jean Piaget, *Structuralism* (New York: Basic Books, 1970), 5. (Original work published 1968). We owe our reconstruction of Piaget's conception of structure to this work.

13. Ibid., 14.

14. Jean Piaget, *The Origins of Intelligence in Children* (New York: International Universities Press, 1952), 3. (Original work published 1936)

15. Ibid., 3-4.

16. Ibid., 6.

17. Ibid., 14.

18. Piaget adds a sixth alternative, biological emergence and phenomenological epistemology in *The Psychology of Intelligence* (London: Routledge & Kegan Paul, 1967), 11-17. (Original work published 1947) The six alternatives are also discussed exclusively in terms of their epistemological aspect in *Introduction à l'épistémologie génétique*, vol. 3 (Paris: Presses Universitaries de France, 1950), 80-120. Piaget found this sixth version inadequate, essentialy because it is a non-developmental theory.

19. Piaget's stages of development can be briefly summarized as follows: 1) *Sensorimotor intelligence* (0-2 years) This stage is characterized by the movement from a reflex level to sensorimotor activity. 2) *Preoperational representations* (2-7 years) Here the first crude symbols, representations, and intuitions appear. 3) *Concrete operations* (7-11 years) The child's conceptual organization takes place by virtue of the formation of cognitive structures called groupings. 4) *Formal operations* (11-15 years) The child can now deal with the possible, the abstract, and the conceptual.

20. Piaget, *The Origins of Intelligence in Children*, 365.

21. Ibid., 375.

22. Ibid., 384.

23. For a concise statement of the similarities between Piaget and Kant see, Richard J. Blackwell, "The Adaptation Theory of Science," *International Philosophical Quarterly* 13 (1973): 333-34.

24. An excellent account of Piaget's epistemological views can be found in John Flavell, *The Developmental Psychology of Jean Piaget* (Princeton, N.J.: Van Nostrand Co., 1963), 67-84. The most comprehensive treatment of Piaget's epistemology is Richard Kitchener, *Piaget's Theory of Knowledge: Genetic Epistemology & Scientific Reason* (New Haven: Yale University Press, 1986).

25. Jean Piaget, *The Construction of Reality in the Child* (New York: Ballantine, 1971), 357. (Original work published 1937)

26. Ibid., 32-38. The details of the process by which schemata transform is described by Piaget in terms of the various types of assimilation. Functional assimilation is the propensity of schemata for repeated application. Generalizing assimilation refers to the tendency of schemata to extend their range of application to new objects. Recognitory assimilation describes the ability of schemata to recognize or differentiate between objects. Finally, schemata are characterized by the tendency to become more complex, what Piaget refers to as reciprocal assimilation.

27. Jean Piaget, *The Construction of Reality in the Child*, 397.

28. Ibid., 401.

29. Ibid., 402.

30. Piaget's knowledge of pragmatism is deficient, since the organism/environment interaction is at the heart of Dewey's naturalism. A more neo-Kantian version is in Pierce's developmental epistemology.

31. A few of Piaget's principle works during this period were: Piaget & Inhelder, *Le développement des quantités chez l'enfant*, 1941. Piaget & Szeminska, *La genése du nombre chez l'enfant*, 1941. Jean Piaget, *Le*

développement de la notion de temps chez l'enfant, 1946. *Les notions de mouvement et de vitesse chez l'enfant*, 1946. Piaget & Inhelder, *La représentation de l'espace chez l'enfant*, 1948. Piaget, Szeminska, and Inhelder, *La géométrie spontanée chez l'enfant*, 1948. And Jean Piaget, *La genése de l'idée de hasard chez l'enfant*, 1951.

32. Jean Piaget, *The Psychology of Intelligence*, (London: Routledge & Kegen, Paul, 1967), 49. (Original work published 1945).

33. Jean Piaget, "Jean Piaget," 256.

Chapter 3

1. References to this fact may be found throughout his writings. To cite just one example, in his conversations with Jean-Claude Bringuier, Piaget claimed, "I'm not a psychologist. I'm an epistemologist." Bringuier. *Conversations with Piaget*, (Chicago: University of Chicago Press, 1977), 49.There is other evidence to support this claim. Consider the title of what may be his magnum opus, *Introduction à l'épistémologie génétique*, or the name of his research institution, The Center for Genetic Epistemology.

2. Jean Piaget, *Introduction à l'épistémologie génétique*, vol. I, (Paris: Presses Universitaires de France, 1950), 13. In W. E. Beth, W. Mays, and J. Piaget, *Épistémologie génétique et recherche psychologique* (Paris: Presses Universitaires de France, 1957), 13.

3. Jean Piaget, *Logique et connaissance scientifique*, (Paris: Gallimard, 1967), 7.

4. Jean Piaget, "Programme et méthodes de l'épistémologie génétique," trans. J. Flavell, 14. See also *Introduction à l'épistémologie génétique*, vol. 1, 12.

5. See John Flavell, *The Developmental Psychology of Jean Piaget*, 251-254. I have developed my description of the scope of genetic epistemology from his account.

6. *Introduction à l'épistémologie génétique*, vol. 1, 38.

7. Ibid., vol. 1, 38-39.

8. Ibid., vol. 1, 39.

9. Ibid., vol. 1, 40.

10. Ibid., vol. 1, 41.

11. Ibid., vol. 1, 42.

12. Ibid., vol. 1, 43.

13. Ibid., vol. 1, 43-44.

14. Ibid., vol. 1, 45.

15. Ibid., vol. 1, 47.
16. Ibid., vol. 1, 47.
17. Ibid., vol. 1, 48.
18. Ibid., vol. 1, 49.
19. See Jean Piaget, *Genetic Epistemology* (New York: Norton, 1970), 10-12.
20. This point is discussed in *The Principles of Genetic Epistemology* (London: Routledge & Kegan Paul, 1972), 73-74. (Original work published 1970) Note also that Piaget's most mature theories of mathematical knowledge are contained in his work with E. W. Beth: *Mathematical Epistemology and Psychology* (Dordrecht: Reidel, 1966).
21. *Introduction à l'épistémologie génétique*, vol. 3, 66.
22. Ibid., vol. 3, 69.
23. Ibid., vol. 3, 70-71.
24. Ibid., vol. 3, 128.
25. Ibid., vol. 3, 273.
26. Ibid., vol. 3, 278.
27. Ibid., vol. 3, 278.
28. Ibid., vol. 3, 305.
29. Ibid., vol. 3, 306.
30. Ibid., vol. 3, 312.
31. Jean Piaget, "Épistémologie génétique et methodologie dialectique," *Dialectica* 4, 293.
32. Jean Piaget, *Logique et équilibre* (Paris: Presses Universitaires de France, 1957), 32.
33. Piaget also made clear his belief that evolution is orthogenetic in *Logique et connaissance scientifique* (Paris: Gallimard, 1967), 116.

Chapter 4

1. A partial list of his publications during this period include: *Understanding Causality* 1971, *The Grasp of Consciousness* 1974, *Success and Understanding* 1974, *Experiments in Contradiction* 1974, and *The Equilibration of Cognitive Structures* 1975. Collaboration with B. Inhelder produced, *Memory and Intelligence* 1968, and *Mental Imagery in the Child* 1966. In addition numerous contributions were made to the multi-volume *Etudes d'épistémologie génétique*.
2. Jean Piaget, "The Genetic Approach to the Psychology of Thought," *Journal of Educational Psychology* 52 (1961), 275-81. See also: "Develop-

ment and Learning," *Journal of Research in Science Teaching* 2 (1964), 176-86, and the conclusion of *The Psychology of the Child* 1966.

3. Jean Piaget, *Biology and Knowledge: An Essay on the Relations of Organic Regulations and Cognitive Processes* (Chicago: University of Chicago Press, 1971), 23. (Original work published 1967) Epigenesis is the theory that the germ cell has no pre-given structure (preformism) and the embryo develops into a new creation through environmental interaction. Henceforth, this is how the term will be used.

4. Ibid., 26.

5. Ibid., 34.

6. Ibid., 26.

7. Ibid., 50-51.

8. Ibid., 51.

9. Ibid., 79.

10. Ibid., 288-96. In a series of footnotes Piaget cited, among others, the following authors: V. Grant, J. M. Baldwin, F. Jacob, C. H. Waddington, and T. Dobzhansky.

11. My account of the biological evidence is taken from Jean Piaget, *Adaptation and Intelligence* (Chicago: University of Chicago Press, 1980), 17-45. (Original work published 1974) In addition, Piaget offers a fine summary of the theory of the phenocopy in: J. C. Bringuier, *Conversations with Jean Piaget* (Chicago: University of Chicago Press, 1980), 110-17. (Original work published 1977)

12. Jean Piaget, *Adaptation and Intelligence*, 73.

13. Ibid., 74.

14. Ibid., 111.

15. Ibid., 119.

16. Ibid., 119.

17. Jean Piaget, *Behavior and Evolution* (New York: Random House, 1978), ix. (Original work published 1976)

18. Ibid., 139.

19. Ibid., 142.

20. Ibid., 147-148.

21. I use the word "teleonomic" to avoid the use of teleological and finalism. My use of the word "teleonomic" follows that of C. H. Waddington and Ernest Mayr. According to Waddington, it does not denote that the end state is external to the process and steers evolution; it is a "quasi-finalistic" term implying only that the process is goal-oriented. See C.H. Waddington, *The Evolution of an Evolutionist* (Ithaca: Cornell University

Press, 1975), 223. Mayr defines teleonomic similarly: A teleonomic process or behavior is one which owes its goal-directedness to the operations of a program." Ernst Mayr, *Toward a New Philosophy of Biology* (Cambridge: Harvard University Press, 1988), 45.

22. Jean Piaget, *Behavior and Evolution*, 151.

23. Ibid., 159.

Chapter 5

1. Thomas Kuhn, *The Structure of Scientific Revolutions* (Chicago: University of Chicago Press, 1962), x.

2. Ibid., 94.

3. Ibid., 157.

4. Ibid., 170-171.

5. Kuhn does offer a metalevel claim for objective criteria of theory choice in his "Objectivity, Value Judgment and Theory Choice," in his *The Essential Tension*. I return to his earlier view for purposes of comparison.

6. Jean Piaget & Rolando Garcia, *Psychogenesis and the History of Science* (New York: Columbia University Press, 1989). I concentrate my reconstruction on Piaget's contributions to this joint effort and, for the sake of simplicity, refer to Piaget only.

7. Ibid., 28-29.

8. Ibid., 109.

9. Ibid., 255.

10. P. K. Feyerband, *Science in a Free Society* (London: New Left Books, 1979).

11. I present Popper as a simple falsificationist. Some commentators, like Lakatos for example, have argued persausively that he is a sophisticated methodological falsificationist. I present the simple view for the sake of comparison.

12. Ibid., 265. Piaget criticized Kuhn—and others who philosophize without any empirical base—on precisely this point. "He [Kuhn] attempts to reconstruct the way a child learns what a duck is without taking the trouble to find out empirically (that is, by observing real children) whether this is really the way children learn. Several years of research with children have shown that children do not, in fact, learn the way Kuhn imagined."

13. Ibid., 274.

14. A previous version of this chapter appeared in *The Modern Schoolman* (volume 73, number 4) as "Psychogenesis and the History of Science: Piaget's Philosophy of Science."

Chapter 6

1. Jean Piaget, *The Child's Conception of Causality*, (New York: Routledge and Kegan Paul, 1930), 240.

2. Jean Piaget, *Genetic Epistemology*, (New York: Norton, 1970), 13.

3. Brian Rotman, *Jean Piaget: Psychologist of the Real* (Sussex, England: Harvester Press, 1977), 60.

4. Alvin Plantinga, "An Evolutionary Argument Against Naturalism," Paper presented for the Wade Memorial Lecture, St. Louis University, St. Louis, Missouri, Feb. 2, 1992. Plantinga argued that it is highly improbable that evolution can account for the reliability of our cognitive faculties. For another case against evolutionary epistemology see: Thomas Nagel, *The View From Nowhere* (New York: Oxford University Press, 1986), 78-82.

5. Donald T. Campbell, "Evolutionary Epistemology," in *The Philosophy of Karl Popper*, Book I, ed., Paul A. Schilpp (La Salle: Open Court, 1973), 413.

6. Boris I. Balinsky, *An Introduction to Embryology*, 3d ed. (Philadelphia: W. B. Saunders Co., 1970), 9. For an interesting discussion of the philosophical implications of the ontogeny-phylogeny relationship see: Jane M. Oppenheimer, *Essays in the History of Embryology and Biology* (Cambridge: The M.I.T. Press, 1967).

7. Stephen Jay Gould, *Ontogeny and Phylogeny* (Cambridge: The Belknap Press of Harvard University Press, 1977), 5.

8. Ibid., 2.

9. Gould's interpretation of Piaget is mistaken. It is the functions—not the structures—which provide the "external constraints" regulating ontogenetic and phylogenetic evolution. Possibly Gould meant to say the structure "at a given time" regulates evolution. But even this is misleading since the structures of mind are continually evolving and are themselves products of the invariant functions. For Gould's discussion of Piaget see: Stephen Jay Gould, *Ontogeny and Phylogeny*, 144-47.

10. Jean Piaget, "Genetic Epistemology," *Columbia Forum* 12 (1969), 4.

11. Jean-Pierre Changeux, "Genetic Determinism and Epigenesis of the Neuronal Network: Is There a Biological Compromise between Chomsky and Piaget?," in *Language and Learning: The Debate between Jean Piaget*

and Noam Chomsky, ed. Massimo Piattelli-Palmarini (Cambridge: Harvard University Press, 1980), 196.

12. Ibid., 196.

13. Ibid., 195.

14. Antoine Danchin, "A Critical Note on the Use of the Term Pheno-copy," in *Language and Learning: The Debate between Jean Piaget and Noam Chomsky*, 357.

15. Ibid., 359.

16. Ibid., 359.

17. Ibid., 360.

18. Jean Piaget, *Six Psychological Studies*, (New York: Random House, 1967), 103-4. (Original work published 1964)

19. Jean Piaget, *The Equilibration of Cognitive Structures*, (Chicago: University of Chicago Press, 1985), 3-4. (Original work published 1975)

20. Ilya Prigogine, *From Being to Becoming*, (San Francisco: W.H. Freeman, 1980). See also Ilya Prigogine and Isabelle Stengers, *Order Out Of Chaos*, (New York: Bantam Books, 1984), 12-14.

21. Jacques Monod, *Chance and Necessity: An Essay on the Natural Philosophy of Modern Biology*, (New York: Alfred A. Knopf, 1971), 112-113.

22. Ibid., 113-115.

23. Hans Furth, *Knowledge as Desire: An Essay on Freud and Piaget*, (New York: Columbia University Press, 1987), 138.

24. B. C. Goodwin, "Genetic Epistemology and Constructivist Biology," *Revue Internationale de Philosophie*, (1982), 537.

Bibliography

Apostel, Leo. "The Unknown Piaget: From the Theory of Exchange and Co-Operation toward the Theory of Knowledge." *New Ideas in Psychology* 4, no. 1 (1986): 3-22.

Atkinson, Christine. *Making Sense of Piaget: The Philosophical Roots.* London: Routledge & Kegan Paul, 1983.

Balestra, Dominic. "Piaget's Genetic Epistemology of Mathematics." Ph.D. diss., St. Louis University, 1977.

_____. "The Mind of Piaget: Its Philosophical Roots," *Thought* 55, 1980.

Bergson, Henri. *Creative Evolution.* New York: Modern Library, 1944. (First published 1907)

Blackwell, Richard. "The Adaptation Theory of Science." *International Philosophical Quarterly* 13 (1973): 319-334.

_____. "A Structuralist Account of Scientific Theories." *International Philosophical Quarterly* 16 (1976): 263-274.

Brief, Jean-Claude. *Beyond Piaget: A Philosophical Psychology.* New York: Teachers College Press, 1983.

Bringuier, Jean-Claude. *Conversations with Jean Piaget.* Chicago: Univ. of Chicago Press, 1980.

Chapman, Michael. *Constructive Evolution: Origins and Development of Piaget's Thought.* Cambridge: Cambridge University Press, 1988.

Cohen, David. *Piaget: Critique and Reassessment.* New York: St. Martin's Press, 1983.

156 *Bibliography*

Feyerabend, P. K. *Science in a Free Society*. London: New Left Books, 1979.

Flavell, James. *The Developmental Psychology of Jean Piaget*. New York: D. Van Nostrand Company, 1963.

Furth, Hans. *Piaget & Knowledge*. 2d. ed. Chicago: University of Chicago Press, 1981.

_____. *Knowledge as Desire: An Essay on Freud and Piaget*. New York: Columbia University Press, 1987.

Gardner, Howard. *The Quest for Mind: Piaget, Levi-Strauss, and the Structuralist Movement*. Chicago: Univ. of Chicago Press, 1972.

Ginsburg, Herbert, and Sylvia Opper. *Piaget's Theory of Intellectual Development*. Englewood Cliffs, N.J.: Prentice Hall, 1969.

Glaserfeld, Ernst von. "Radical Constructivism and Piaget's Concept of Knowledge." In F. B. Murray, ed. *Cognitive Psychology: The Impact of Piaget*. New York: Plenum Press. pp. 109-22.

_____. "An Interpretation of Piaget's Constructivism." *Revue Internationale de Philosophie*, (1982): 612-35.

Goodwin, B. C. "Genetic Epistemology and Constructionist Biology." *Revue Internationale de Philosophie*, (1982): 527-48.

Gould, Stephen Jay. *Ontogeny and Phylogeny*. Cambridge: The Belknap Press of Harvard University Press, 1977.

Gruber, H., and J. J. Voneche, eds. *The Essential Piaget*. New York: Basic Books, 1977.

Gutting, Gary. *Paradigms and Revolutions*. South Bend: University of Notre Dame Press, 1980.

Hahlweg, K., and C. A. Hooker, eds. *Issues in Evolutionary Epistemology*. Albany: SUNY Press, 1989.

Hamlyn, D. W. *Experience and the Growth of Understanding*. London: Routledge & Kegen Paul, 1978.

Haroutunian, Sophie. *Equilibrium in Balance: A Study of Psychological Explanation*. New York: Springer-Verlag, 1983.

Kitchener, Richard. *Piaget's Theory of Knowledge*. New Haven: Yale University Press, 1986.

Kuhn, Thomas. *The Structure of Scientific Revolutions*. 2d. ed. Chicago: University of Chicago Press, 1970.

_____. "Reflections on My Critics." In *Criticism and the Growth of Knowledge*. Cambridge: Cambridge University Press, 1970.

Lakatos, Imre. "Falsification and Methodology of Scientific Research Programs." In *Criticism and the Growth of Knowledge*. Cambridge:

Cambridge University Press, 1970.

Mayr, Ernst. *Toward a New Philosophy of Biology.* Cambridge: Harvard University Press, 1988.

Meyerson, Emile. *Identity and Reality.* New York: Dover Publications, 1962. (Original work published 1908)

Mischel, Theodore. *Cognitive Development and Epistemology.* New York: Academic Press, 1971.

Modgil, Sohan, and Celia Modgil, eds. *Jean Piaget: an Interdisciplinary Critique.* London: Routledge & Kegen Paul, 1983.

Monad, Jacques. *Chance and Necessity: An Essay on the Natural Philosophy of Modern Biology.* New York: Alfred Knopf, 1971.

Nagel, Thomas. *The View from Nowhere.* New York: Oxford University Press, 1986.

Oppenheimer, Jane. *Essays in the History of Embryology and Biology.* Cambridge: The M.I.T. Press, 1967.

Phillips, John. *The Origins of Intellect: Piaget's Theory.* San Francisco: W. H. Freeman and Company, 1969.

Piaget, Jean. *La mission de l'idée.* Lausanne: La Concorde, 1916.

_____. *Recherche.* Lausanne: La Concorde, 1918.

_____. *The Language and Thought of the Child.* New York: World Publishing Co., 1973. (Original work published 1923)

_____. *Judgment and Reasoning in the Child.* London: Routledge & Kegen Paul, 1928. (Original work published 1924)

_____. *The Child's Conception of the World.* New York: Harcourt, Brace, 1929. (Original work published 1926)

_____. *The Child's Conception of Physical Causality.* New York: Harcourt, Brace and Co., 1930. (Original work published 1927)

_____. *The Moral Judgment of the Child.* New York: Free Press, 1965. (Original work published 1932)

_____. *The Origins of Intelligence in Children.* New York: Norton, 1952. (Original work published 1936)

_____. *The Construction of Reality in the Child.* New York: Ballantine, 1971. (Original work published 1937)

_____. "Intellectual Evolution." In *Science and Man*, ed. R. Anshen, New York: Harcourt, Brace, 1942.

_____. *Plays, Dreams and Imitation in Childhood.* New York: Norton, 1962. (Original work published 1945)

_____. *Psychology of Intelligence.* Routledge & Kegen Paul: London, 1967. (Original work published in 1947)

_____. *Introduction à l'épistémologie génétique*. Vol.1: *La pensée mathématique*. Paris: Presses Universitaires de France, 1950.

_____. *Introduction à l'épistémologie génétique*. Vol. 2: *La pensée physique*. Paris: Presses Universitaires de France, 1950.

_____. *Introduction à l'épistémologie génétique*. Vol. 3: *La pensée biologique, la pensee psychologique et la pensee sociologique*. Paris: Presses Universitaires de France, 1950.

_____. "Épistémologies Génétique Et Methodologies Dialectique II." *Dialectical* 4 (1950): 287-95.

_____. "Jean Piaget". In E. G. Boring, et al., eds., *A History of Psychology in Autobiography*. vol. 4, Worchester, Mass.: Clark University Press, 1952.

_____. *Logic and Psychology*. New York: Basic Books, 1957. (Original work published 1953)

_____."Logique et équilibre dansles comportements du sujet." In L. Apostel, B. Mandlebrot, and J. Piaget, eds., *Logique et équilibre*. Paris: Presses Universitaires de France, 1957.

_____. *Intelligence and Affectivity*. Palo Alto: Annual Reviews Inc., 1981. (Original work published 1954)

_____. *Six Psychological Studies*. New York: Vintage, 1967. (Original work published 1964)

_____. *Insights and Illusions of Philosophy*. New York: Meridian Books, 1971. (Original work published in 1965)

_____. *Biology and Knowledge: An Essay on the Relations between Organic Regulations and Cognitive Processes*. Chicago: University of Chicago Press, 1971. (Original work published 1967)

_____. *Logique et connaissance scientifique*. Paris: Gallimard, 1967.

_____. *Structuralism*. New York: Basic Books, 1970. (Original work published in 1968)

_____. *Épistemologie des sciences de l'homme*. Paris: Gallimard, 1970.

_____. *The Principles of Genetic Epistemology*. London: Routledge & Kegen Paul, 1972. (Original work published 1970)

_____. *Main Trends in Psychology*. New York: Harper, 1973. (Original work published 1970)

_____. *Genetic Epistemology*. New York: Norton, 1970.

_____. "Chance and Dialectic in Biological Epistemology: A Critical Analysis of Jacques Monod's Theses." In W. F. Overton and J. McCarthy Gallaher, eds., *Knowledge and Development*, vol. 1: *Ad-*

vances in Research and Theory. New York: Plenum, 1977. 1-16. (Original work published 1971)

_____. "Intellectual Evolution from Adolescence to Adulthood." *Human Development* 15, (1972): 1-12.

_____. *The Grasp of Conscousness*. Cambridge: Harvard University Press, 1976. (Original work published 1974)

_____. *Adaptation and Intelligence*. Chicago: University of Chicago Press, 1980. (Original work published 1974)

_____. *Success and Understanding*. Cambridge: Harvard University Press, 1978. (Original work published 1974)

_____. *Experiments in Contradiction*. Chicago: University of Chicago Press, 1980. (Original work published 1974)

_____. *The Development of Thought: Equilibration of Cognitive Structures*. New York: Viking, 1977. (Original work published 1975)

_____. *Behavior and Evolution*. New York: Pantheon, 1978. (Original work published 1976)

_____. "Problems of Equilibration." In M. H. Appel and L. S. Goldberg, eds., *Topics in Cognitive Development*, vol. 1: *Equilibration: Theory, Research, and Application*. New York: Plenum, 1977. pp.3-13.

_____. *Possibility and Necessity*, vol. 2, *The Role of Necessity in Cognitive Development*. Minneapolis: University of Minnesota Press, 1987. (Original work published 1983)

Piaget, J., and E. W. Beth *Mathematical Epistemology and Psychology*. Dordrecht: Reidel, 1966. (Original work published 1961)

Piaget, J., and B. Inhelder *The Psychology of the Child*. New York: Basic Books, 1969. (Original work published 1966)

Piaget, J., and R. Garcia *Psychogenesis and the History of Science*. New York: Columbia University Press, 1989. (Original work published 1983)

Piattelli-Palmarini, M., ed. *Language and Learning: The Debate between Jean Piaget and Noam Chomsky*. London: Routledge & Kegen Paul, 1980.

Prigogine, Ilya. *From Being to Becoming*. San Francisco: W. H. Freeman, 1980.

Prigogine, Ilya, and Isabelle Stengers. *Order out of Chaos*. New York: Bantam Books, 1984.

Pulaski, Mary Ann. *Understanding Piaget*. New York: Harper & Row, 1980.

Popper, Karl. *The Logic of Scientific Discovery*. London: Hutchinson,

1962.

_____. *Objective Knowledge*. Oxford: Oxford University Press, 1972.

Radnitzky, G., and W. W. Bartley, eds. *Evolutionary Epistemology, Rationality, and the Sociology of Knowledge*. LaSalle, Il: Open Court, 1987.

Rotman, Brian. *Jean Piaget: Psychologist of the Real*. Bristol, England: Harvester Press, 1977.

Schilpp, Paul Arthur, ed. *The Philosophy of Karl Popper*. La Salle: Open Court, 1974.

Silverman, J., ed. *Piaget, Philosophy, and the Human Sciences*. Atlantic Higlands, N.J.: Humanities Press, 1980.

Spencer, Herbert. *First Principles*. 6th ed. Akron: Werner Co., 1900. (Original work published 1862)

Waddington, C. H. *The Evolution of an Evolutionist*. Edinburgh: Edinburgh University Press, 1975.

Wadsworth, Barry. *Piaget's Theory of Cognitive Development*. New York: Longman Inc., 1971.

Wuketits, Franz, ed. *Concepts and Approaches in Evolutionary Epistemology*. Dordrecht: D. Reidel Publishing Company, 1984.

Index

About the Author

John G. Messerly (Ph.D. Saint Louis University) is assistant professor of philosophy at Ursuline College in Pepper Pike, Ohio. His published works have appeared in: *International Philosophical Quarterly; Kinesis; The Modern Schoolman; Philosophical Studies; The Review of Metaphysics;* and *Southwest Philosophy Review*, among others. In addition, he is the author of *An Introduction to Ethical Theories* (Lanham, Md.: University Press of America, 1995).